CW01191928

JEAN GENIUS

JEAN GENIUS

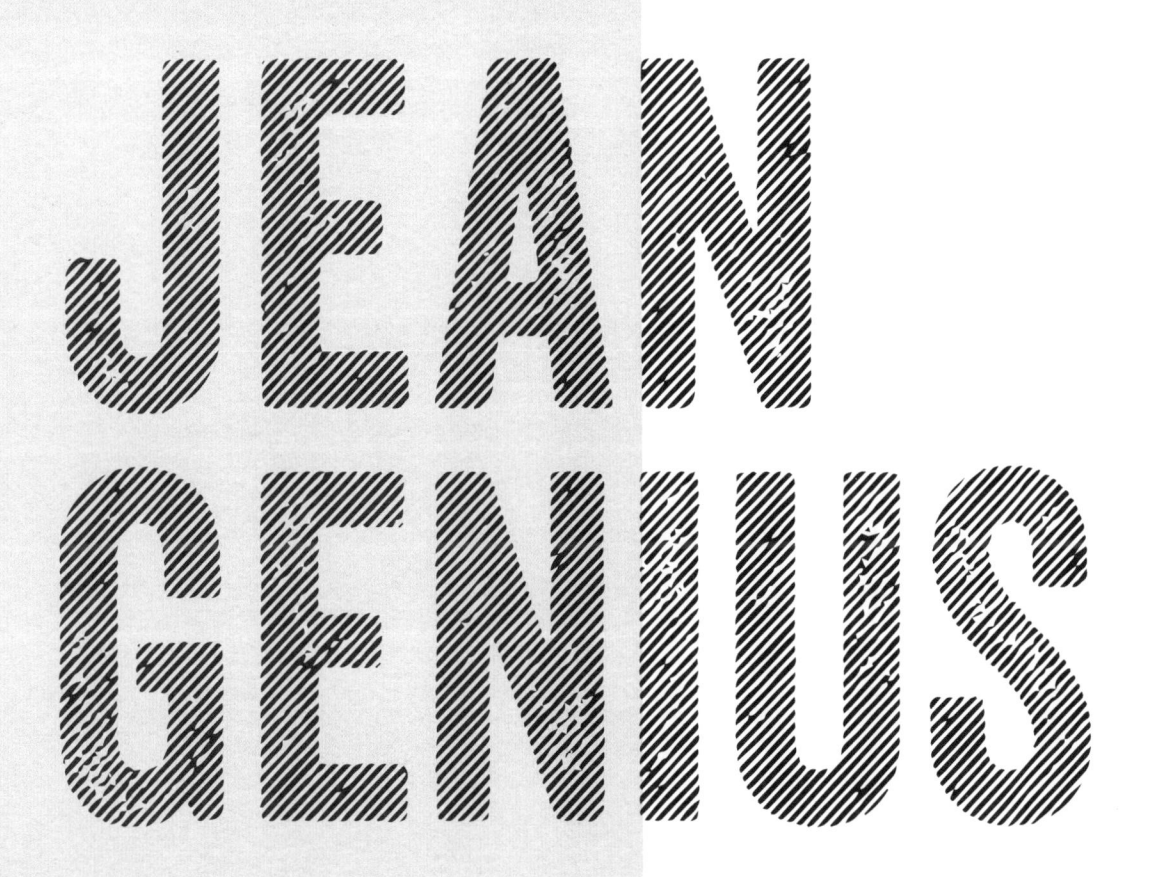

REPAIR, RESTYLE AND REPURPOSE YOUR DENIM

JANELLE HANNA

Skittledog

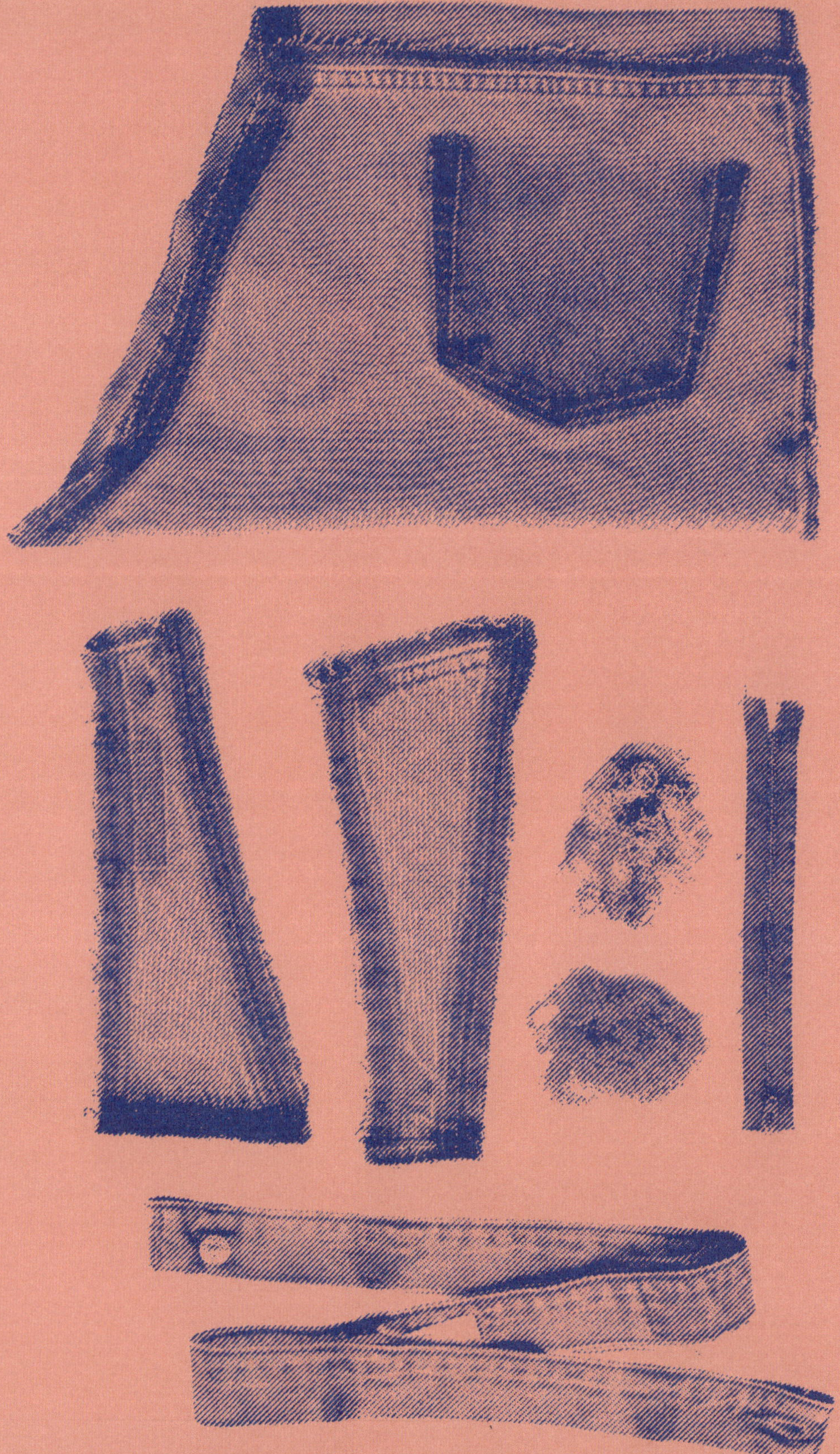

CONTENTS

	The slow-denim revolution	07
	What is denim?	08
	The importance of indigo	11
	The ecological footprint of a pair of jeans	12
	How to become a jean genius	16
KNOW-HOW	Tools & equipment	25
	Jeans anatomy	30
	Full jeans deconstruction	33
	Taking your jeans apart	34
	Tips for sewing with denim	39
REPAIR	Darning	47
	Patching	55
	Hand-stitched repairs	65
	Altering hems	77
RESTYLE	Adding leg inserts	85
	Jeans to shorts	97
	Jeans to skirt	103
REPURPOSE	Reversible sunhat	113
	Scrap patch pouch	121
	Patchwork market bag	127
	Visor	133
	Slippers	141
	Patchwork	149
	Resources	156
	About the author / acknowledgements	158

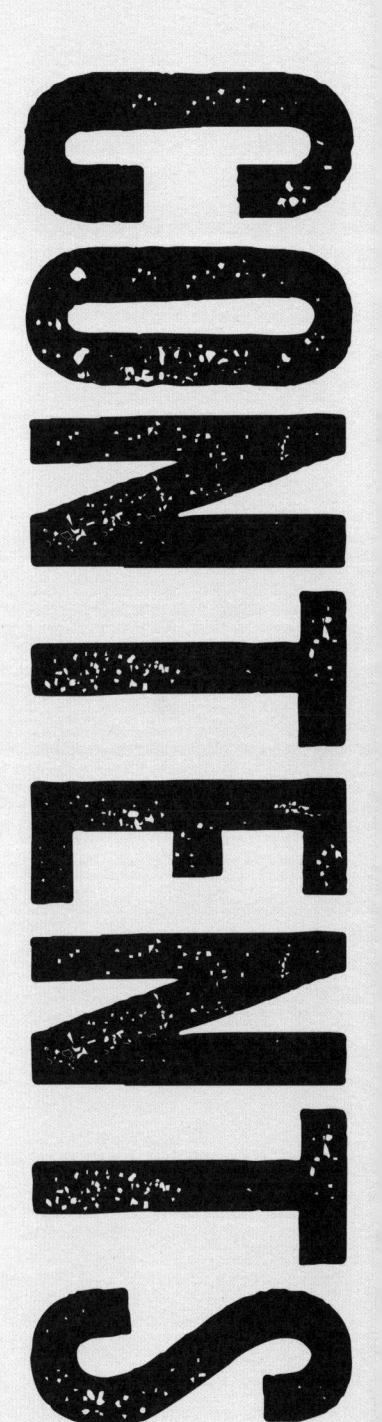

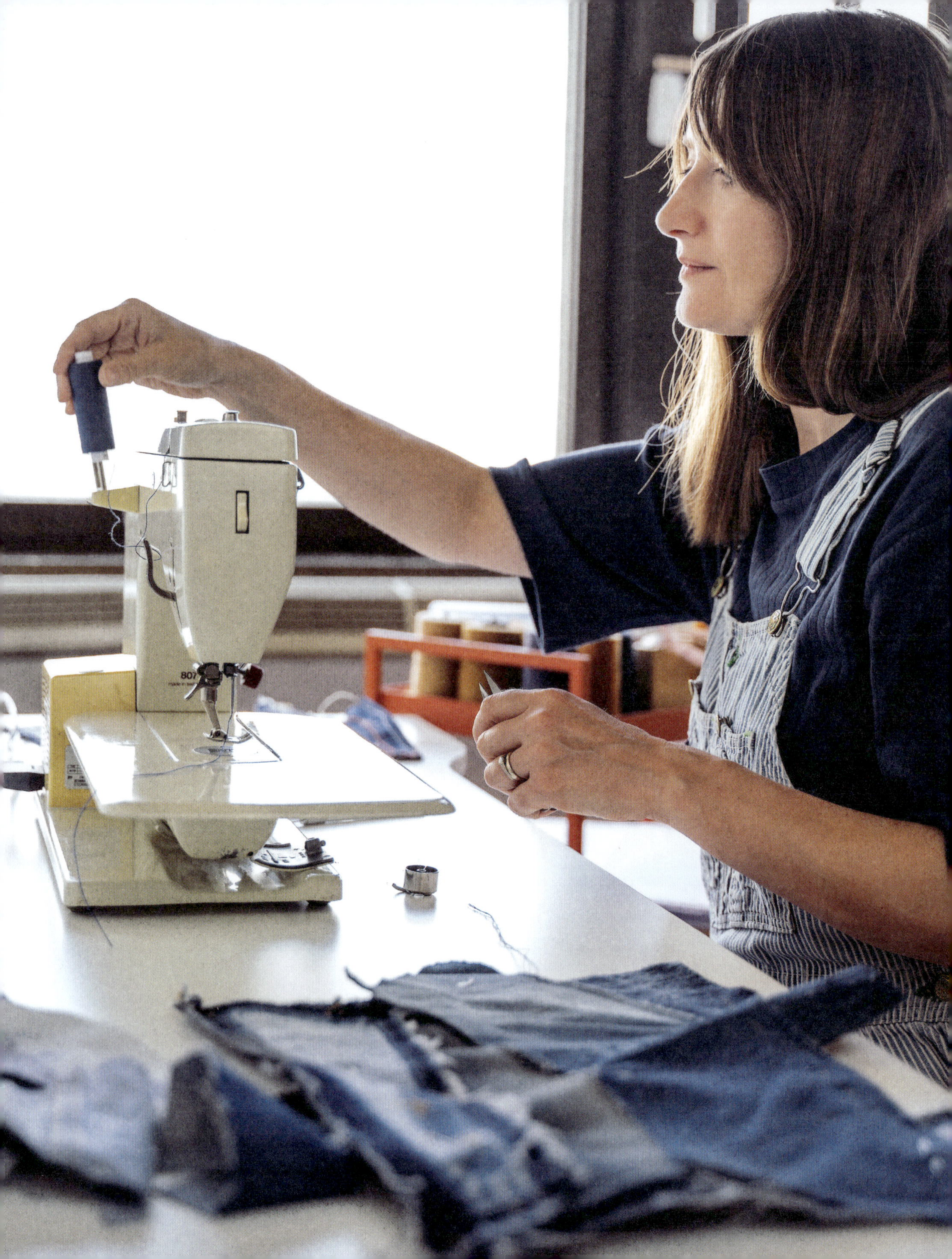
807

My fascination with denim began as a child when the side seam on my friend's stonewashed jeans split, revealing a sliver of dark indigo beneath the faded fabric. That unexpected glimpse of hidden colour sparked a curiosity that would only grow in the decades to come.

THE SLOW-DENIM REVOLUTION

Fast forward ten years to when, on the cusp of starting a fashion design degree at university, I landed a work placement at one of the UK's last remaining denim factories, which happened to be in my home town. From that moment, fascinated by the magic I witnessed as dark cloth was transformed to blue jeans, I was hooked on indigo.

I was drawn to the honesty and inclusivity of jeans, as well as their cultural cache, rich heritage and creative potential. But as my career in the fashion industry progressed and I found myself designing collections for iconic global brands, I couldn't ignore the harsh reality behind the scenes. The alchemy of indigo dyeing that had initially captivated me came at a steep cost.

Modern denim production is a chemical-intensive process, consuming thousands of litres of water and vast amounts of energy to achieve the faded looks we've grown accustomed to. And with most denim now containing synthetic fibres, recycling can be challenging. Adding to the problem is the staggering overproduction of jeans. With an estimated 4.5 billion pairs of jeans churned out each year for a global population of 8 billion, we're drowning in denim.

It was against this backdrop of excess and climate concern that I founded White Weft in 2015. The mission was clear: to rebel against the fashion industry's relentless pace and actively encourage a slower, more mindful relationship with what we wear. Surrounded by the waste of my own design work, I began creating accessories from denim swatches and jeans diverted from recycling centres. It soon became apparent that most discarded jeans were still in great condition, save for a few rips and tears, a realization that inspired me to open our studio doors to repairs.

Having straddled both sides of denim – as a designer and repairist – I bring a unique perspective to crafting lasting repairs and professional-looking upcycled products. My passion and hope for this book are to share these skills, because if we're to challenge the fast-fashion industry, home repair and sewing skills must be part of the revolution.

So, if you've ever felt intimidated by sewing denim, fear not! This book is your guide, filled with projects that will breathe new life into your jeans and empower you to make them last for years to come. Let's stitch our way into a more sustainable and creative future.

WHAT IS DENIM?

Before you dive into working with denim, it can be helpful to understand what makes this fabric unique. Its distinct weave, rich history and manufacturing process all shape how it behaves and ages when used in garments. With a bit of background knowledge, you'll make more informed decisions when repairing, altering or sewing with denim.

The origin story of denim goes all the way back to 17th-century France, where it got its name from the phrase *serge de Nîmes*, meaning 'fabric from Nîmes'. Back then it was a lighter-weight material, made from wool blended with other fibres and dyed with indigo, and it was mostly used to make over-garments for manual labourers.

The popularity of this durable cloth spread. Eventually it made its way to the US (via the UK), where cotton replaced wool, and denim fabric more similar to what we know today was created. The ubiquitous blue jeans were born in post-Gold Rush San Francisco in 1873, when fabric merchant Levi Strauss and tailor Jacob Davis added copper rivets to utility trousers to make them stronger.

For decades blue jeans were a practical staple worn primarily by miners and cowboys, a fact that changed only in the 1950s when Hollywood icons like Marlon Brando and James Dean adopted the look on screen. In an instant, this humble work garment was transformed into a symbol of youthful rebellion and effortless cool. From bell-bottoms to skinny jeans, denim's appeal has constantly morphed but never faded. But what makes it different from your everyday cotton fabric? What makes denim, denim?

WEAVING PATTERNS

Denim is a woven fabric. If you're unfamiliar with textile terms, that means it's made by interlocking horizontal and vertical fibres, called yarns, by weaving them together on a loom. The vertical yarns are called the warp and the horizontal yarns are the weft.

`A distinguishing feature of true denim, is that it has an indigo-dyed warp and a white, undyed weft.`

For added strength, thick yarns are used in a 3 x 1 twill construction, a special kind of weaving pattern. Lightweight fabrics like shirting or wool tailoring have a weaving construction where each weft yarn will pass over one warp then under one. However, for denim the weft yarns pass over one warp, then under three warps, making the cloth stronger and softer than a plain weave and creating the distinctive diagonal surface effect.

`Indigo warp`   `White weft`

WHAT IS DENIM MADE FROM?

Until the arrival of stretch denim in the mid-1970s, most jeans were made of 100% cotton. Nowadays, the vast majority of jeans are made from stretchy denim containing synthetic fibres blended with cotton. If you check the label, you may find any of these fibres in your jeans.

- Cotton: coming from the fluffy seedpods of the cotton plant.
- Elastane (or Spandex in the US): a stretchy polymer that comes from petroleum.
- Polyester: a common synthetic fibre that comes from petroleum and is added to denim to lower the cost and to aid the stretchability.
- Viscose, modal and lyocell: sometimes added to denim for softness. These types of fibres are man-made but not synthetic as they come from the processing of natural materials from sources such as trees, bamboo or other plants.

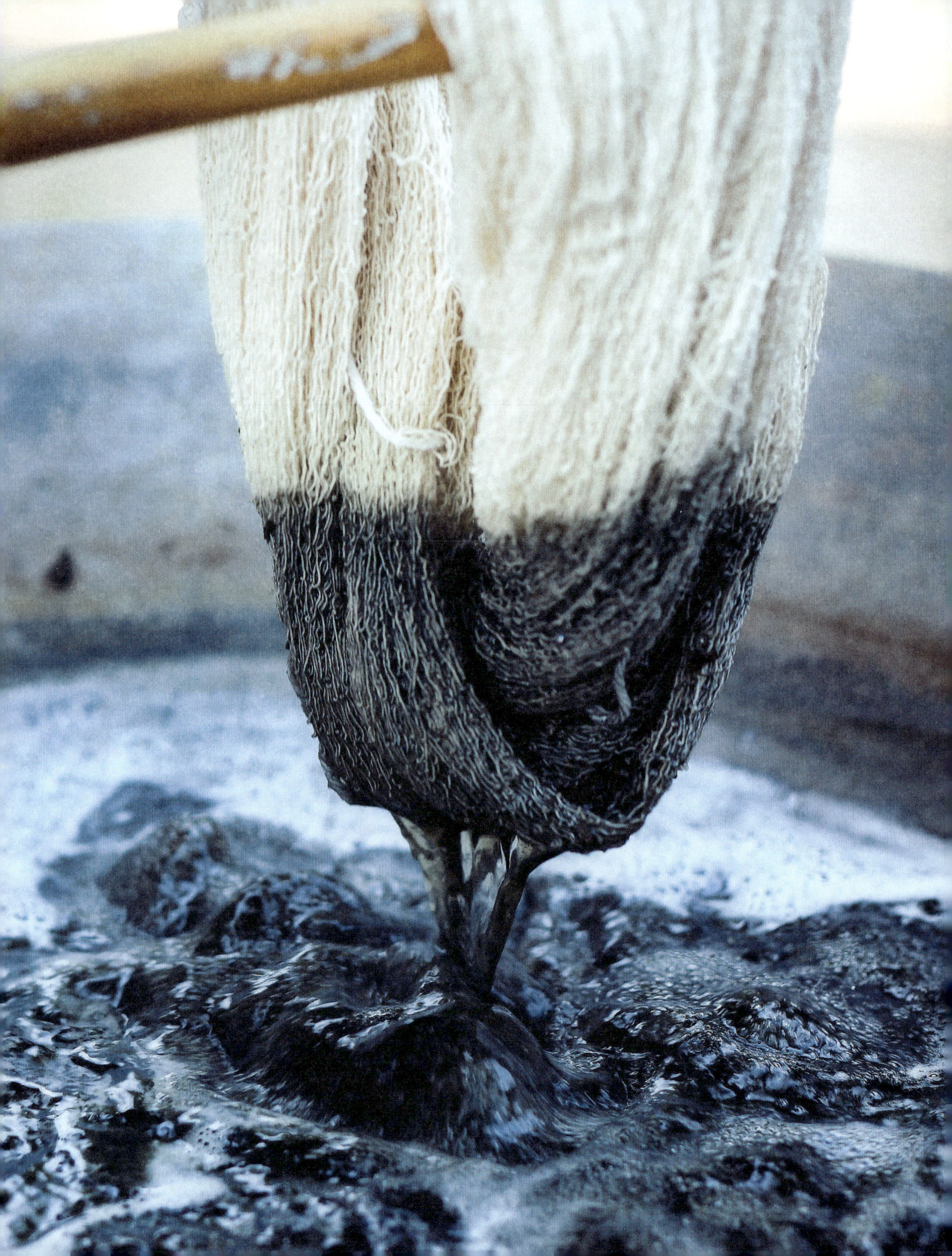

THE IMPORTANCE OF INDIGO

So far, I've described a historically important fabric with a specific weaving construction. But without the magic ingredient, indigo, it would still be a plain old twill. Like many denim enthusiasts, my own fascination stems from the effects of the indigo dye and the mysterious inky ripples of colour that appear as a garment ages.

HOW DOES INDIGO WORK ITS MAGIC?

Indigo dye originally comes from plants, most famously *Indigofera,* which is native in many tropical regions. There are also other varieties such as woad that can grow in cooler places. Humans have been dyeing with indigo for thousands of years. Blue is a spiritual colour and an elusive hue in the natural dye palette, and so indigo was revered and even attributed with a mystical status in many ancient cultures.

Adding to this intrigue is that the dye itself is actually invisible, locked inside the green leaves of the plant. It is only through a specific sequence of actions and reactions that the blue dye emerges. The process is mesmerizing to watch, as liquid indigo touches the cloth, first colouring it pale green then slowly morphing to blue when exposed to the air, which allows the dye to oxidize.

But patience is required to achieve those illustrious midnight shades as the cloth must be soaked in the dye bath and hung out to air multiple times. Layers of dye build up, and the colour deepens with each immersion. Believe it or not, this is true even of the industrial indigo dye process used to make our jeans today. Sadly, the scale and speed of modern denim production means that natural plant-based indigo is rarely used. Instead, the dye in your jeans is likely to be a synthetic chemical replica of *Indigofera* dye.

FADE EFFECTS

Whether plant dye or synthetic, indigo retains its unique and distinctive fade effects. Other dye types change over time but they age in a more even and subtle way. Vintage denim fades so uniquely, giving us clues to the life and habits of its previous owners. For example: bright, chalk-like streaks resulting from being hung on a fence in the sun; oil marks and worn knees from manual labour; or unusual wear on a specific place, such as the strap marks on a guitarist's jacket.

The reason for this is down to its chemical composition and, more precisely, its relationship with cotton. Indigo dye molecules do not have a good bond with cotton so rather than fully submerging the yarn, the dye sits on the surface. Over time, the colour chips off, revealing the white core of the yarn in unique patterns that reflect the bodies and movements of the wearer.

While the most beautiful fade effects are created through natural authentic wear, most denim today is pre-faded by industrial laundries as a short cut to this worn-in look. Denim fabrics always begin as a dark, almost black, shade; the range of mid- and light-blue jeans is achieved with chemical washing and distressing techniques. If not done responsibly, this process involves toxic chemicals, thousands of litres of water and can be harmful to workers.

When it comes to sustainability, denim can actually be a great choice for your wardrobe – but only if we approach it with the right mindset. Jeans are tough, versatile and can outlive most other clothing if you take good care of them. But it's important to remember just how much goes into making a single pair of jeans and the impact that has on people and the planet.

THE ECOLOGICAL FOOTPRINT OF A PAIR OF JEANS

WATER PRESERVATION

Producing a single pair of jeans can use an average of 7,000–10,000 litres (1,850–2,650 gallons) of water for irrigating the cotton crop (less than 30% of cotton is rain-fed) to dyeing the fabric and creating those faded looks. This depletes local water supplies where the denim is made, often in water-stressed countries such as Bangladesh, Pakistan and China.

Once used, the water becomes contaminated and if not cleaned properly it is hazardous to humans and marine life when released into the rivers. Brands and governments in the Global North have been to slow to take responsibility for this. On the positive side, it is perfectly possible to vastly reduce the water imprint of denim. Technology exists that can reduce, clean and even eliminate the use of water if brands and customers are willing to pay for it.

CHEMICAL OVERLOAD

What won't be listed on your jeans label is the long list of chemicals used in the manufacturing process, many of them hazardous. While they may not reach toxic thresholds on the jeans we end up wearing, campaigners warn of darker consequences for factory workers and the environment.

From the moment the cotton seed is planted, most jeans rely on petrochemicals. Growing cotton as a monocrop for the past 50 years has starved the soil of nutrients, making farmers reliant on synthetic fertilizers and pesticides to supercharge its growth. The fall-out is a drastic reduction in biodiversity; water contamination coming from the fields; illness amongst farming communities and a crisis in soil health that puts future generations at risk of food shortage.

One alternative is regenerative farming, which follows methods that are non-toxic and improve the soil health and biodiversity. Denim made from regenerative cotton is now a reality and offers hope for the soil. You can also reduce the impact of the cotton in your jeans by choosing certified organic or jeans containing recycled cotton.

Then there are the plethora of chemicals used to make the cotton into jeans. Potassium permanganate, also known as PP, is used on the majority of jeans sold in the European Union and US to create fade effects. It's usually applied manually with a spray gun. Workers exposed to PP are known to suffer skin irritation, respiratory problems and long-term organ damage. PP is hazardous to marine life when released into rivers and can accumulate in the food chain. Today many brands claim to be phasing out this nasty chemical. Alternatives exist, such as fading with laser etching or using less toxic bleaching agents, but fast fashion continues to prioritize profit and speed and so PP remains in widespread use.

There are many other chemical compounds in our jeans: sodium hypochlorite, aniline, sodium hydrosulphite, to name a few; even something as innocuous sounding as the salts used in the dyeing process, if released into waterways, can disrupt ecosystems with disastrous effects.

STONEWASHING

Most people have heard the term stonewashing used to describe the mottled denim effect, heavily associated with jeans of the 1980s and 1990s. As the name suggests, it's achieved by tumbling the jeans in a huge washer with thousands of tiny bleach-soaked stones. What most people don't consider is where these stones come from and most would be surprised to learn they are actually mined from hillsides all over the world from Mexico to Turkey.

It takes over 1.5kg (3.3lb) of pumice stones to wash one pair of jeans. After a few uses they begin to crumble and need to be replaced so great chunks of mountainside are scooped out at a rapid rate. Besides this ludicrous loss of natural resources, the powdery residue from the stones soaks up a chemical soup from the washing process, creating a toxic sludge that becomes another environmental hazard if not disposed of safely. Responsible brands and factories will now be eliminating stonewashing or replacing stones with longer-lasting (most often plastic) alternatives.

WORKERS' WELFARE

It's unfortunately no secret that the fashion industry does not offer a dignified wage to the majority of garment workers. While most brands claim to pay the legal minimum wages of the country they manufacture in, the reality is that wages in most manufacturing countries are poorly regulated and fall far below a liveable standard where workers can afford the basics of life such as food, shelter, healthcare and education for their children. Living wages for garment workers are so rare they're practically non-existent.

Denim is not an exception. While new legislation in the EU will hold brands accountable for wage and human rights violations in their producer's factories, this safeguards legal wages, not living wages and only extends so far; workers further down the chain, for example in the cotton farms and ginneries where cotton is processed, remain extremely vulnerable to exploitation, not excluding forced labour and child labour.

All clothing is handmade, in the case of a pair of jeans, made by many hands perhaps across a number of continents.

PURCHASING POWER

If you're buying new jeans, these small tips can make a big difference:

- Look out for jeans certified by Blue Sign, GOTS or The Jeans Redesign for increased confidence that toxic chemicals have not been used.
- If you want a pair of stonewashed jeans, only buy no-stone or pumice-free versions.
- Try looking for brands that share wage information and list the names of their producers.
- Look for mention of living wages; you should be able to find their sustainability or Environmental, Social and Governance (ESG) policies on the brand's website.

THE PROBLEM OF WASTE

We've reached a place where 4.5 billion new pairs of jeans are being produced every year. But where do the old ones go? This isn't just a case of overstuffed wardrobes – it's a huge global problem.

When we donate clothing to charity or take it to a clothing bank, we somehow hope what isn't resold is going to be re-spun and reincarnated as a cute eco T-shirt but the harsh reality is that right now only 1 per cent of clothing is recycled into new garments. The rest gets put into landfill, incinerated or down-cycled into products like insulation and single-use wiping rags, or shipped off for resale in another country.

Every year, huge volumes of discarded fast-fashion clothing are being exported to countries in the Global South from Europe and the US, supposedly for resale in the second-hand markets, but the flow now exceeds the demand as the quality of the clothing has steadily deteriorated over the past decade. Places like Accra in Ghana and the Atacama Desert in Chile have become dumping grounds for our fast-fashion cast-offs. Journalists report how mountains of old clothes are piling up in waterways and fragile ecosystems, overwhelming local communities who don't have the resources to manage all this waste. Most brands do nothing to clean up the mess of their overproduction.

As one of the most popular clothing items on earth, denim plays no small part in the problem, especially when we consider the types of fabrics in most of today's jeans. Because they contain synthetics, a pair of stretch jeans can take hundreds of years to fully decompose. During that time, they break down into microplastics, leeching into the soil and water, and entering the local food chain.

The cost of a pair of jeans weighs much heavier than the material we hold in our hand and the price on the tag. It's this value we must keep in mind as we buy use and dispose of our denim with care.

JEANS GENERATE 2.16 MILLION TONS OF WASTE PER YEAR*

*Luiken and Bouwhuis Recovery and recycling of denim waste, 2015.

HOW TO BECOME A JEAN GENIUS

If you have gone to the trouble of researching and investing in more ethical and sustainable jeans, you'll want to keep them going for as long as possible.

I'm often asked about recycling and where to donate clothes to avoid them being dumped in the Global South or incinerated. There's no easy answer to this. I always advise people to try to redistribute clothing locally by offering it for free on neighbourhood groups or giving it to a local charity such as a refuge or clothes bank. If a garment is damaged, consider mending it before passing it on. But by far the best action we can take is to buy well and keep wearing, repairing and reinventing the clothing we have. If we all did this, the volume of clothing waste would be a fraction of what it currently is.

With the skills you will pick up from this book you'll rarely need to contribute to this waste. Visible mending or adapting the fit can breathe new life into old denim. And, when you eventually decide to part ways with a pair, think about how they can be passed on, or repurposed into something completely different.

My final piece of advice is don't hold back! Often people are afraid to ruin their jeans but if something goes wrong you can always add a repair detail. Embrace imperfection as you develop your skills and remember that even the most disastrous project can be revived as a patchwork.

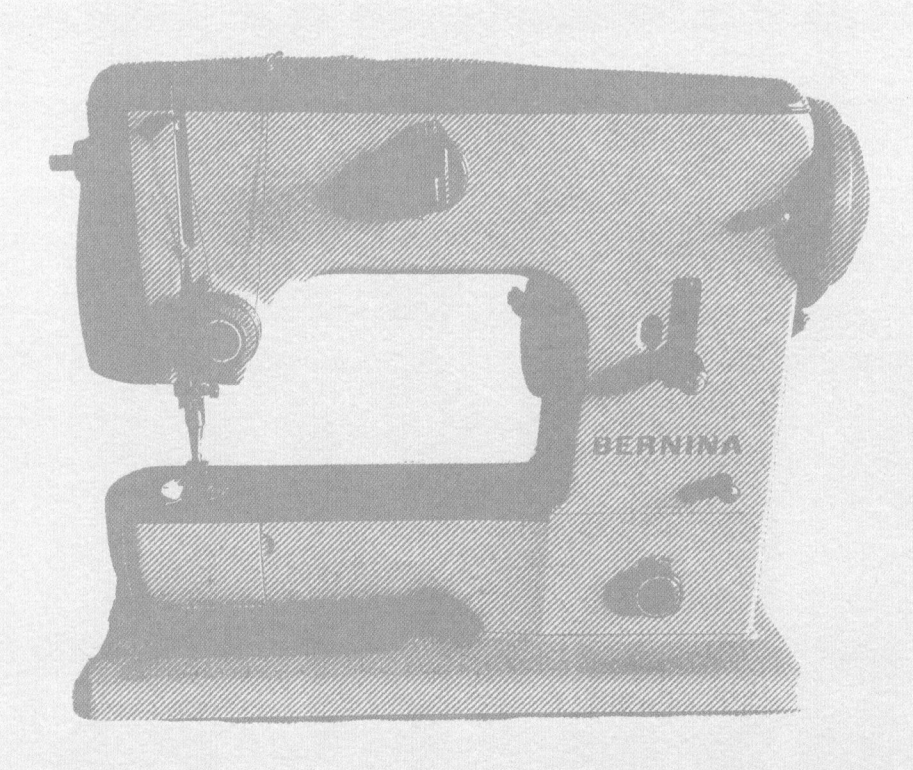

MINING YOUR JEANS
A single pair of jeans holds endless creative possibilities. In our studio, we mine our jeans down to the last scrap. Panels become smaller products and mending patches, useful details such as buttons zips and waistbands are salvaged for future projects.

YOUR JEANS ARE TOO VALUABLE TO END UP AS RAGS

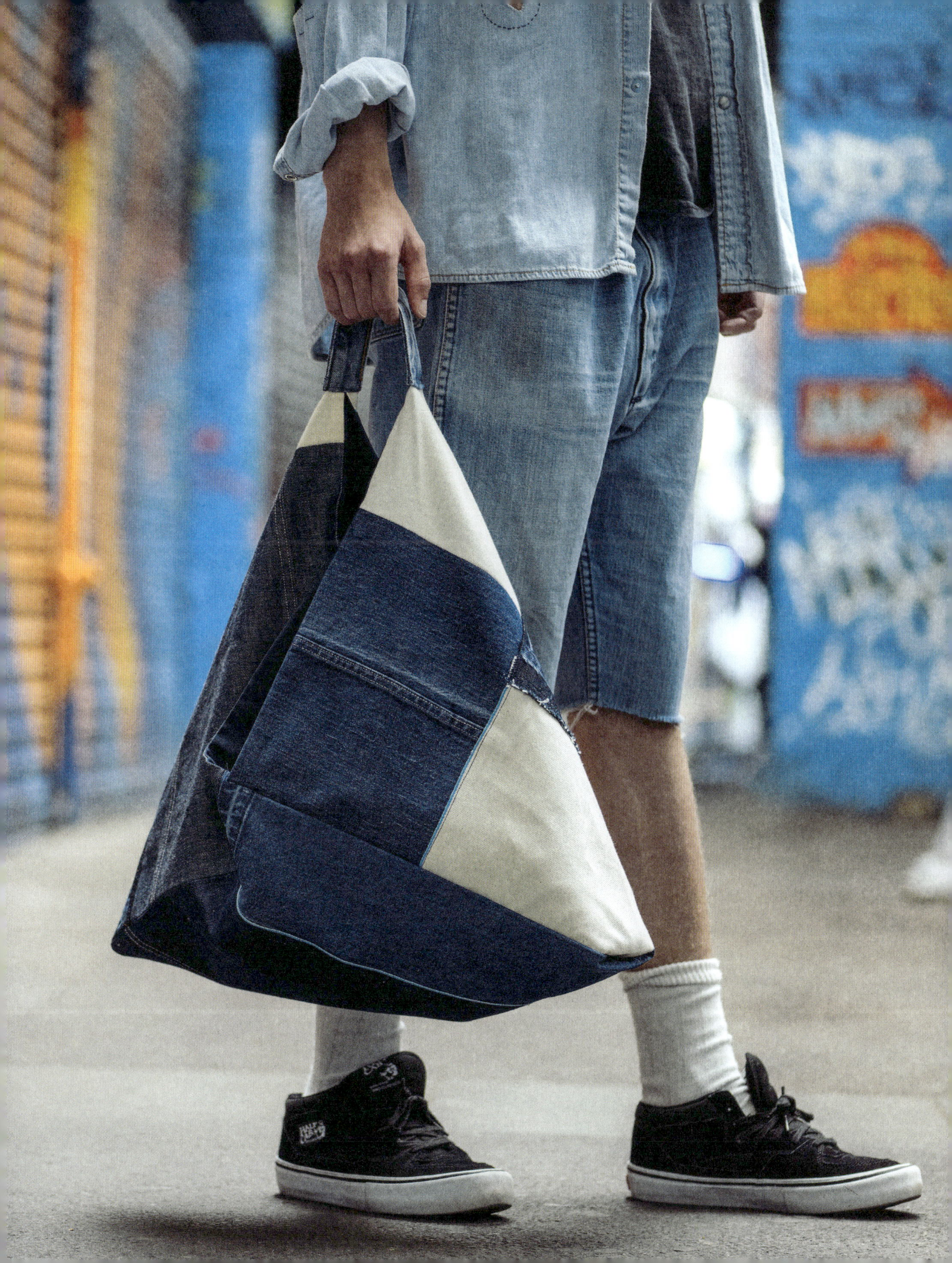

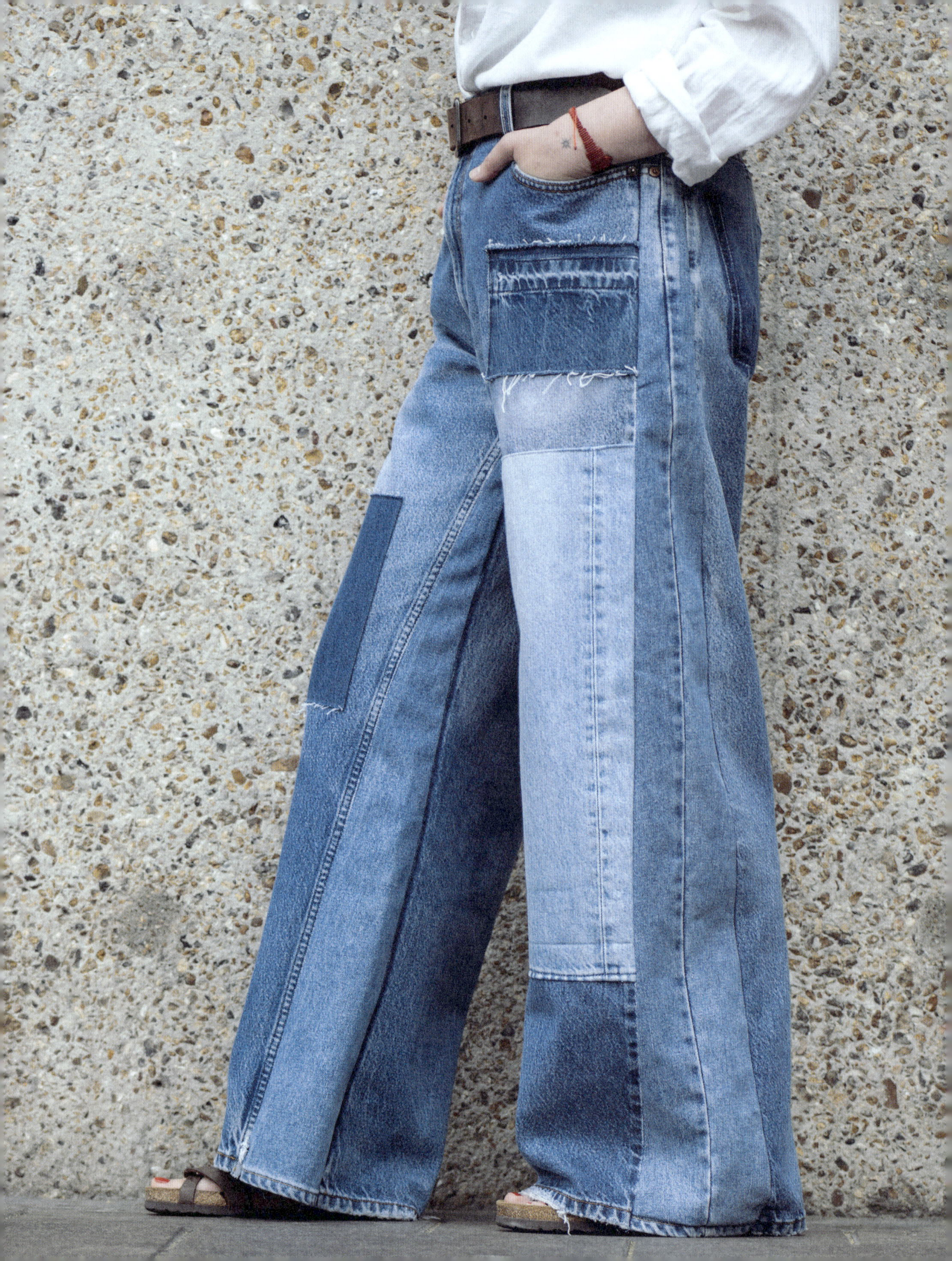

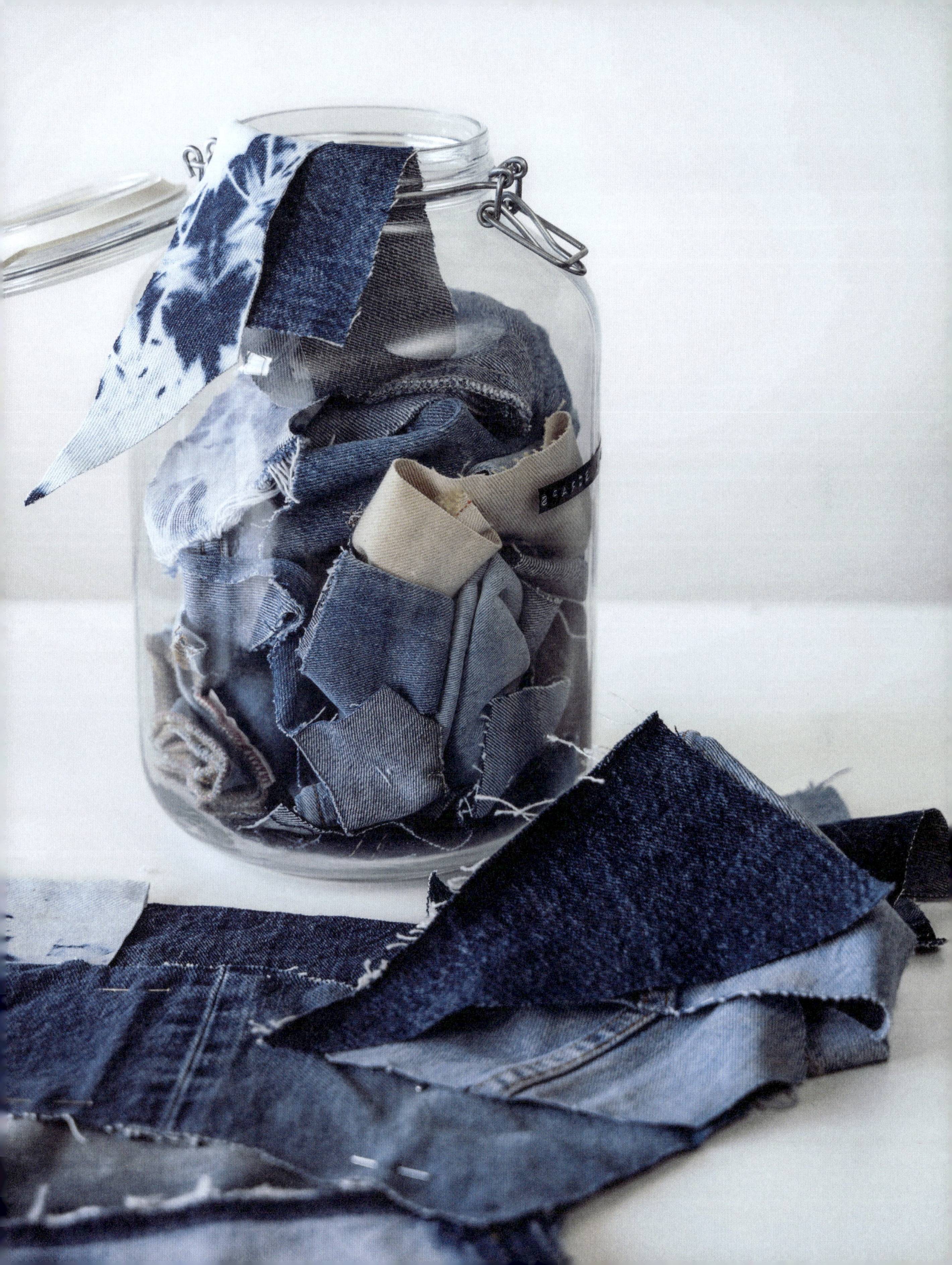

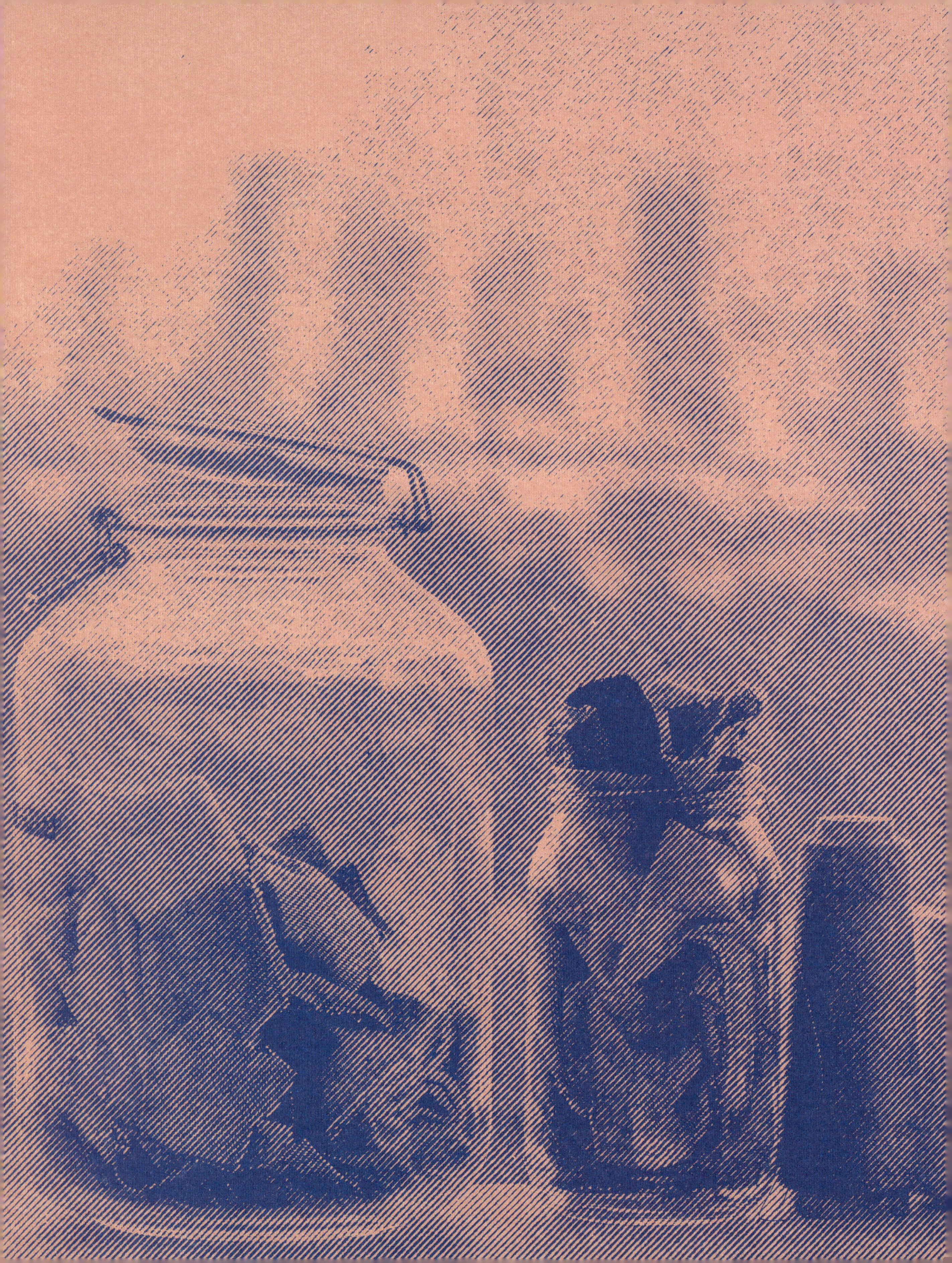

KNOW-HOW

Denim has a reputation for being difficult to sew, but in my experience, the opposite is true. It can be surprisingly forgiving to work with; thicker materials absorb and disguise minor wobbles, and mistakes can be easily unpicked and resewn without damaging the fabric. Over time, I've come to realize that success doesn't require exceptional skill but rather the right tools and an understanding of how to set up the sewing machine for the job.

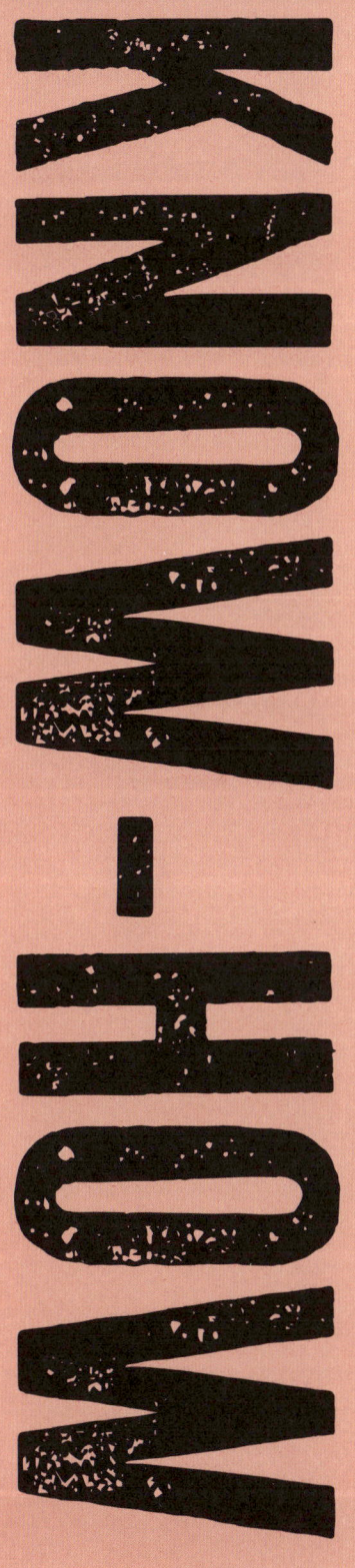

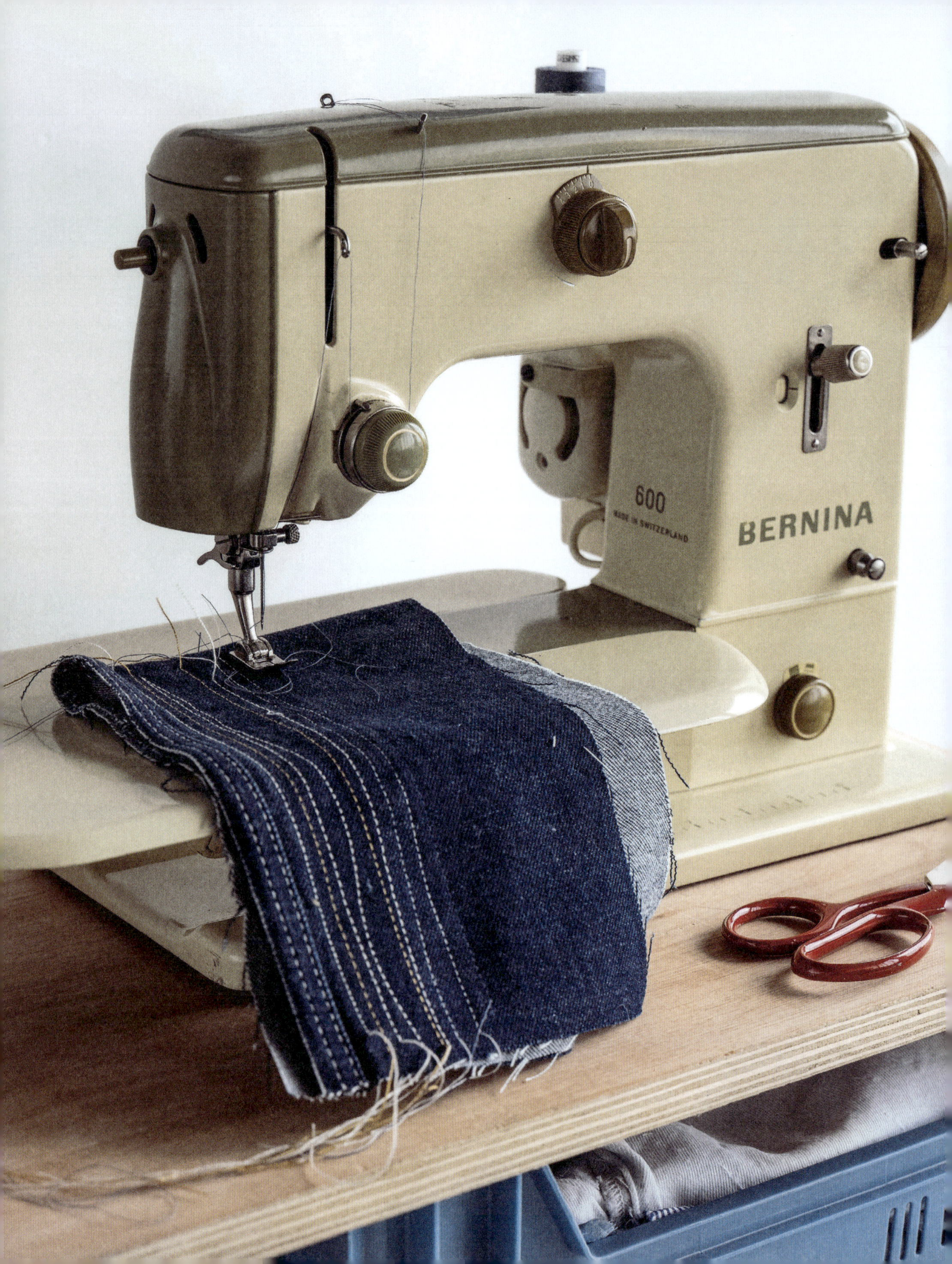
600
MADE IN SWITZERLAND
BERNINA

TOOLS & EQUIPMENT

CHOOSING A SEWING MACHINE

Many of the projects in this book, like darning, patching and adding inserts, can be done on any sewing machine. It's only when you're tackling thick, multi-layered felled seams or hems that some basic models might struggle. If that happens, try the tips on page 39 before considering upgrading your machine.

Personally, I'm a fan of vintage machines, especially models from the 1970s and early 1980s. They tend to have strong motors and sturdy metal bodies, although they are heavier than today's lighter plastic models. Modern machines, while often less durable, have the advantage of being more portable and usually come with an impressive array of automated stitch settings. These features can be handy if you want to try embroidery, quilting or dressmaking with a variety of fabrics.

In the studio, we rely on two vintage Berninas from the 1970s and 1980s. They stitch beautifully and handle thick fabrics almost as well as industrial machines. One of the features I love is the removable sewing bed, which makes it easy to repair sleeves and legs without having to open the seams. One of our machines only does straight and zigzag stitches, but that's more than enough for most of the sewing we do and for all the projects in this book.

KEY FEATURES TO LOOK FOR
If you're thinking about buying a sewing machine, here are things to look for that will make sewing denim easier:

- **A strong motor:** Check for specifications mentioning thick fabrics or heavy-duty sewing.
- **Vintage machines:** Research the brand and ensure parts and servicing are available. Test if possible or buy from a trusted seller online.
- **Stitch options:** Look for machines that have adjustable stitch length.
- **Drop-feed setting:** This can be helpful for repairing with freehand darning.

ESSENTIALS FOR WORKING WITH DENIM

CUTTING

1	Fabric shears
2	Thread snips
3	Seam ripper
4	Scalpel
5	Paper scissors

MEASURING

6	Tape measure
7	Set square or pattern master
8	Ruler

MARKING

9	Tailor's chalk
10	Fabric markers
11	Pencil

SEWING

-	Sewing machine
12	Zipper foot
13	Denim sewing machine needles*
14	Hump jumper
15	Pins
16	Sewing clips
17	Embroidery hoop
18	Sashiko needle
19	Hand-sewing needle
20	Thimble
21	Pin cushion

PRESSING

-	Good-quality steam iron
-	Ironing board
22	Chopstick or point pusher
23	Hammer

THREADS

24	All-purpose threads
25	Heavy-duty topstitch threads
26	Sashiko thread

*(at least a size 90/14 & for thicker denim use a 100/16)

27

CUTTING

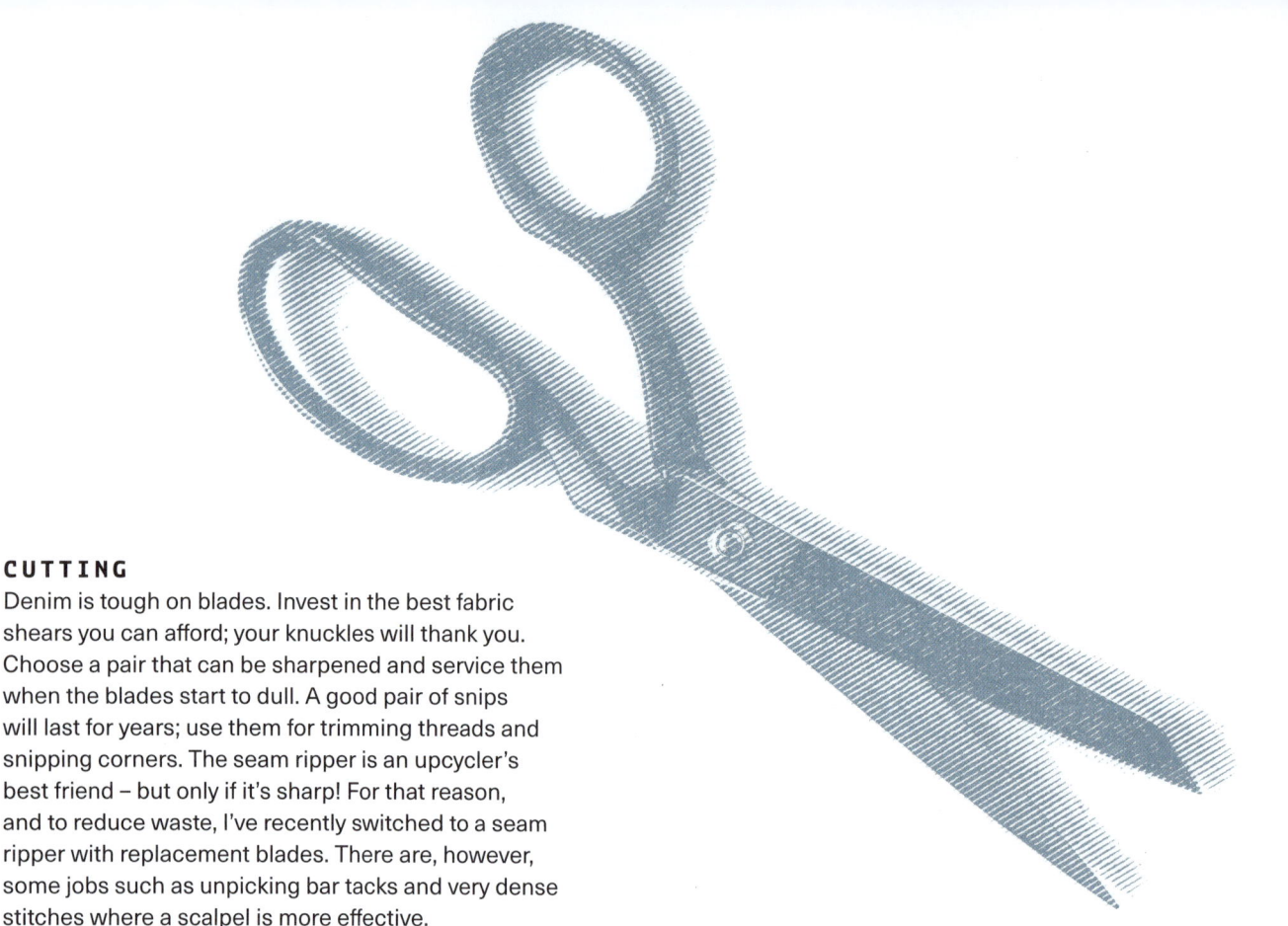

Denim is tough on blades. Invest in the best fabric shears you can afford; your knuckles will thank you. Choose a pair that can be sharpened and service them when the blades start to dull. A good pair of snips will last for years; use them for trimming threads and snipping corners. The seam ripper is an upcycler's best friend – but only if it's sharp! For that reason, and to reduce waste, I've recently switched to a seam ripper with replacement blades. There are, however, some jobs such as unpicking bar tacks and very dense stitches where a scalpel is more effective.

MEASURING

Most of the measuring tools you'll need for these projects are basic household items like a tape measure, ruler or set square. A pattern master is incredibly useful for measuring and marking seam allowances as well as for plotting grain lines and curves.

MARKING

I like to have a variety of marking tools for different surfaces and colours of denim. Tailor's chalk is great on sturdy denim but softer stretchy denim can be difficult to mark with chalk. A marker will come in handy for this and more delicate work such as plotting out hand repairs. We use a fabric marker that disappears with steam or water. On many projects it's fine to mark with a regular pen or wax crayon as you won't see the markings once the pieces are cut and seams are sewn.

MACHINE NEEDLES AND ACCESSORIES

Sewing machine needles come in a variety of sizes for different types of materials. Thick denim should be sewn with 100/16 needles, often marketed as denim needles. Mid-weight denim can be sewn with 90/14 and a universal needle will do for denim shirting. As far as machine accessories, a zipper foot will be useful for sewing in awkward areas and a bulky seam aid helps when sewing through bumpy thick seams.

PINS AND CLIPS

Dressmaking pins are mostly sufficient for prepping seams. It's important that they are sharp and strong. Avoid fine or very long pins for denim projects as they will bend. Some areas are impossible to pin, such as jeans hems or thick layers of patchwork. For this reason, I like to have a few sewing clips handy as well.

THREADS
Our studio is always well stocked with multi-purpose thread in a variety of denim shades for sewing, tacking and darning. The most useful are navy, mid-blue and pale blue, off-white and charcoal grey. If you're planning to sew denim regularly, I'd recommend keeping some pre-threaded bobbins in a variety of shades.

Topstitch thread is not essential for strength but it does help to give the authentic jeans look we expect from denim. The most useful colours are tan, navy and off-white.

You can find topstitch thread in most haberdashery stores in limited colours. They tend to be 100 per cent polyester but if you shop online you can also find 100 per cent cotton topstitch thread.

PRESSING
I stand by the old saying that a good iron is a tailor's best friend. You'll need one with strong steam pressure (the heavier the better for denim) and an ironing board to get the most out of your denim projects. A chopstick or point pusher will help keep corners and edges neat, while a hammer can be used to flatten out bulky seams.

HAND SEWING
A lot can be achieved with a very basic sewing kit. I'd recommend buying or making a needle holder to stop those hand needles from straying. For hand mending, I prefer to use a Sashiko needle; a thimble is advisable for longer projects. Sashiko threads are available in a wide range of colours. I tend to stick to the more traditional blues and off-whites but there are no rules. A small darning hoop can be helpful for some mends, particularly on sleeves or legs, as it keeps the work taut and the front piece away from the back, making it easier to stitch. For me a pincushion is essential. I make mine from scraps and stuff it with fluff or thread trimmings.

JEANS ANATOMY

- Belt loops
- Chainstitch
- Stud button
- Rivet
- Coin pocket
- Lockstitch or straight stitch
- Pocket scoop
- Fly
- J-stitch
- Side seam (or outseam)
- Inside leg seam (or inseam)
- Selvedge seam
- Cuff
- Hem

Back yoke

Waistband

Jeans patch, usually made from leather, plastic or Jacron

Bar tack

Patch pocket

SEAM TYPES

Felled seam

Overlocked seam

Open seam

32

FULL JEANS DECONSTRUCTION

YOU WILL NEED

- Fabric shears
- Thread snips
- Seam ripper
- Scalpel
- Rivet cutters

Disassembling a pair of jeans is time consuming but incredibly satisfying. The first steps can be frustrating and tedious and it's not until the last moment when you've excavated all the threads and removed the final components that the beauty of what remains is finally revealed. There's no shortcut to obtaining those lovely indigo seam shadows and besides your denim panels, you'll be left with lots of great components to use in your upcycling projects, such as zips, pockets and a waistband that can be used as a handle or strap.

With experience, I've managed to reduce the time it takes to fully deconstruct a jean by hours. I want to share my technique to help you get maximum mileage out of all the useful parts in your jeans and get more people upcycling. Even if you only need one component it's really worth trying a complete deconstruction for the insight it offers on how jeans are made. It's an excellent learning exercise for any student or enthusiast.

TAKING YOUR JEANS APART

If you're doing a full deconstruction, completing the steps in the order shown below will speed things up. Before starting, read through the detailed disassembly instructions over the following pages.

I tend to leave the front pocket bags attached to the pocket scoops as they are more useful like that, but you can remove them if required.

FULL DECONSTRUCTION ORDER

1. Open the hems
2. Open the inside leg seam
3. Remove the waistband
4. Open side seams
5. Open centre back seam
6. Remove yokes
7. Remove back pockets
8. Open the front seam / remove fly zip
9. Remove rivets (optional)
10. Remove belt loops

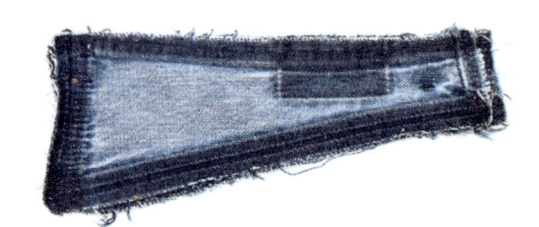

34

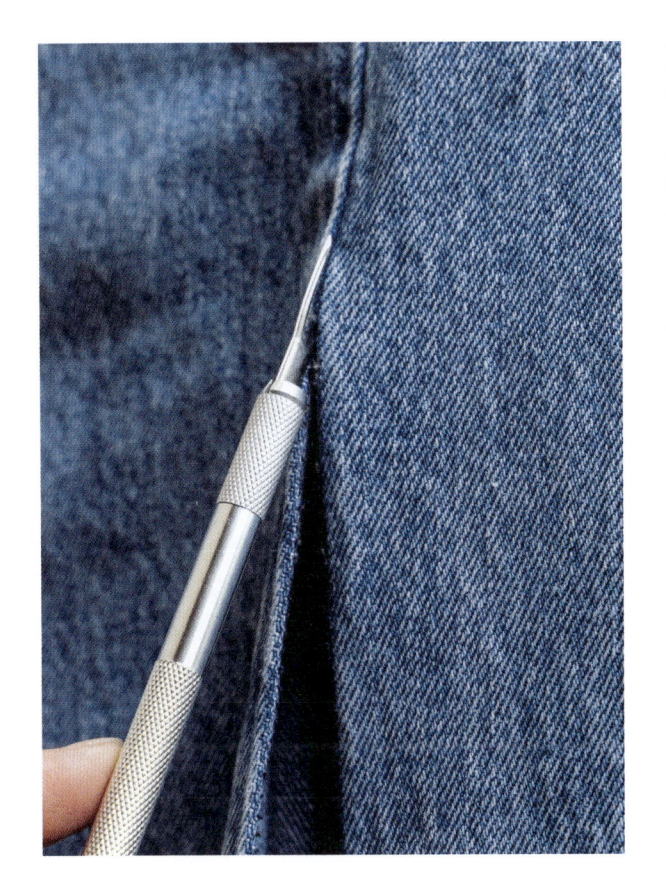

OPENING SEAMS

Use the seam ripper to open overlocked and lock-stitched/straight-stitched seams.

HOW TO USE THE SEAM RIPPER

First unpick three or four stitches with the long end then push the short end into the gap and run the blade through the seam. Gently open areas of dense backstitching by cutting the stitches one by one. If the stitches are very tight for the seam ripper, you can place a scalpel blade between the two layers of fabric and use a gentle sawing motion to break the stitches, taking care not to damage the fabric.

> As the threads come off in long pieces, you can collect them for hand-mending projects or as a filling for stuffed goods.

HOW TO UNDO CHAINSTITCH

Chainstitch can be unravelled in one go by releasing the chain in one satisfying motion, but you must pull the thread in the correct direction. To discover the direction of the chain, first release four or five stitches midway on the seam, using the seam ripper. Pull on the loose thread at the back to see what direction it runs in. If it doesn't unravel in either direction, break a few more stitches to give it some help. Sometimes you have to pull quite hard as dust gathers in the seams and jams the chain. It's also important to check if the chain has been overstitched by a bar tack or backstitch; if that is the case, move clear of that area and try again.

Many leg seams, waistbands, hems, back rise and yoke seams are chainstitched and can be quickly undone, so it's really worth persisting with this technique until you've got the hang of it.

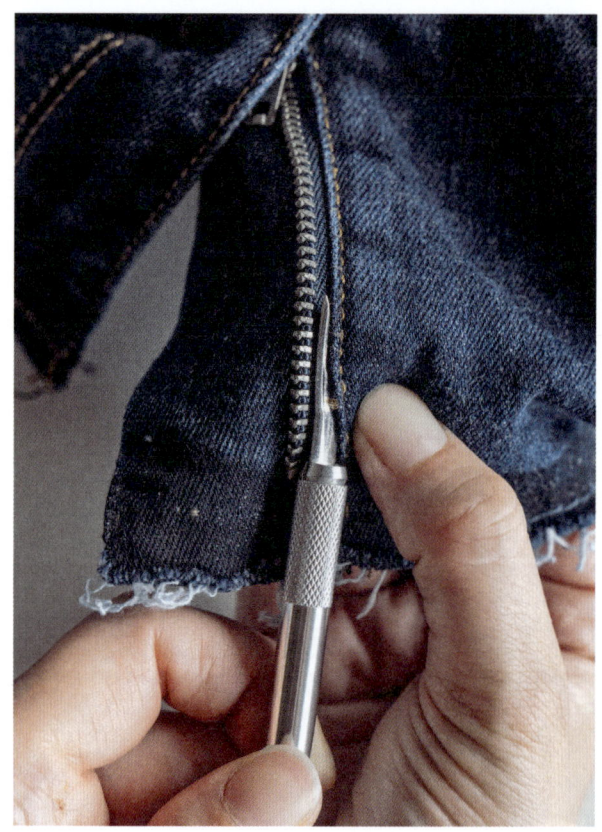

REMOVING BAR TACKS

A scalpel is game changing for removing bar tacks. For years I used a seam ripper, often resulting in stabbed fingers and punctured denim. By placing a sharp scalpel blade between the layers of fabric, you can easily slice through the bar tack. Prise the fabric layers apart as much as possible to reveal the stitches and gently slice or saw through. It should not take a lot of force. If the blade becomes blunt, you need to push more on the scalpel and the process becomes dangerous, so keep the blades sharp.

Removing belt loop bar tacks is even easier. Place the blade between the two sides of the belt loop and slice through the stitching. This way, the blade never touches the jeans, keeping the denim surface intact.

SALVAGING A ZIPPER FROM THE FLY

Remove the waistband first. Use the seam ripper carefully, with the short end to run through the stitches to avoid ripping the zip tape. There are usually two bar tacks on the fly; use the scalpel gently to release them.

REMOVING THE BACK POCKETS

Back pockets are extremely useful for adding to bags and garments so it's always worth saving them.

Use the seam ripper to open the bottom point of the pocket. Unless the fabric is very thin, I usually pull to rip the rest of the stitching. This has rarely torn the denim but if you are concerned, use the seam ripper. Finally, use the scalpel to remove the bar tacks, trying if possible to place the blade between two layers of the pocket rather than between the pocket and the jeans.

REMOVING RIVETS AND JEANS BUTTONS

I seldom need to remove rivets but occasionally do so in order to repair a pocket scoop. If you find you need to remove a rivet or button, you can do so using rivet cutters, which are available at most DIY stores. Rivet cutters are large pliers. Grip the nail at the back side of the button or the rivet with the teeth of the cutters, and squeeze. You may need to rotate the piece and try again from a different angle. Eventually the nail will break or pop out and you can remove all the pieces. It's worth noting that this often damages the back side of fabric.

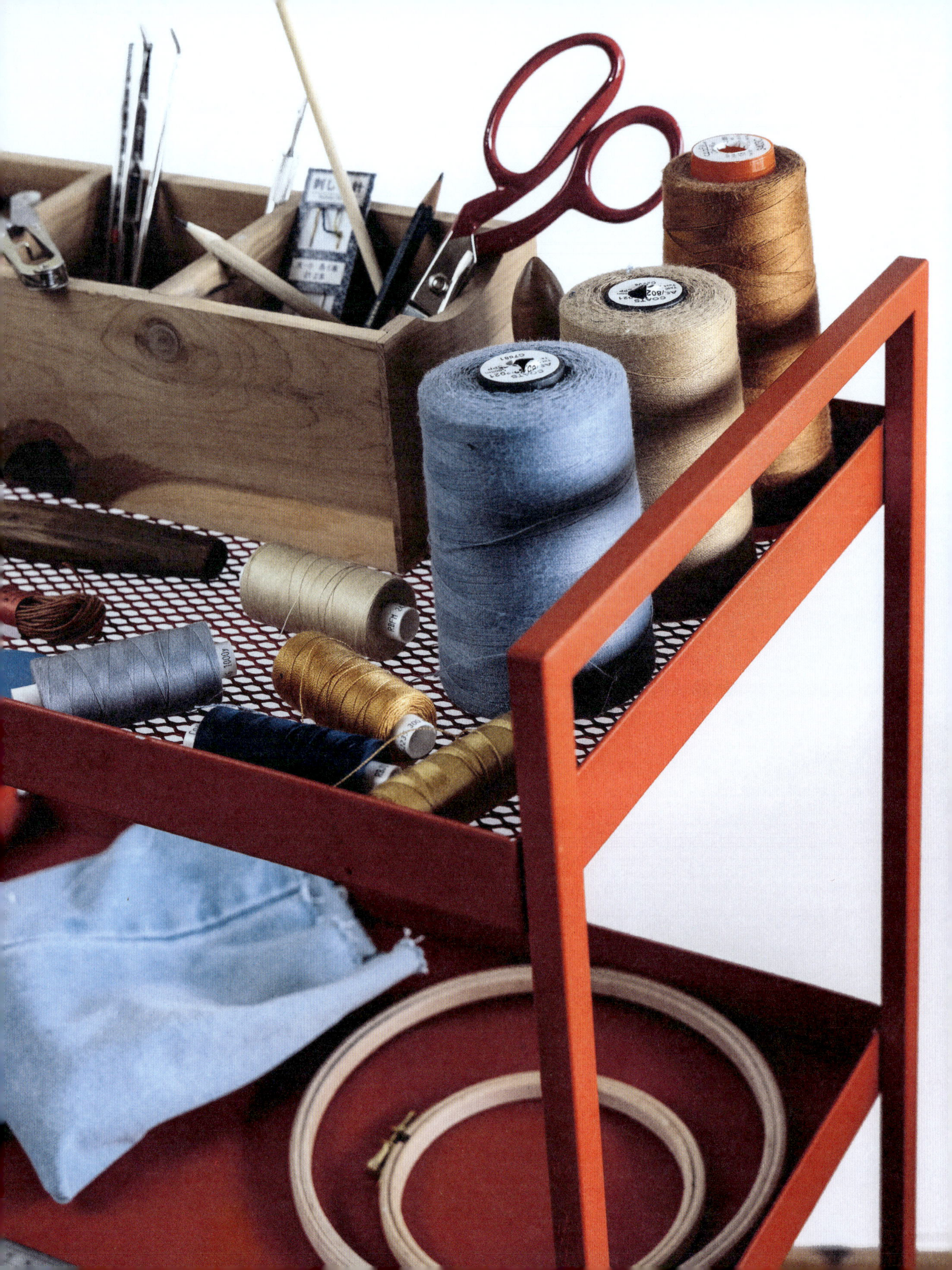

TIPS FOR SEWING WITH DENIM

It can be extremely frustrating when things go wrong with the sewing machine. I've found it massively helpful to understand a bit more about the machine and equipment in order to problem solve when the inevitable happens. With a bit of knowledge, mishaps don't have to mean 'game over'!

PERFECT STITCHING

It's not always necessary to use a thick thread to sew denim. I tend to use a 90/14 needle, universal thread and a stitch length of 3 for all sewing other than topstitching.

For topstitching use heavy-duty topstitching thread and a needle size 100/16 or a specific denim needle. A stitch length of 3.5–4 will give you a look as close as possible to factory-stitched jeans. You will usually need to reduce the top thread tension slightly to account for the thicker thread. Test the stitching as you adjust.

Always test your stitching on a scrap first, making sure to sew through at least two layers – but if you are hemming, sewing or topstitching, remember to test your stitching on the same number of layers as your garment requires.

TROUBLESHOOTING

UNEVEN, WOBBLY & MISSED STITCHES
- Check that the needle is sharp, straight and screwed in tightly. Make sure you are using the correct needle for your thread thickness as a needle eye that's too big or too small can cause problems, as can blunt, twisted or bent needles.

LOOPED STITCHES
- If bobbin loops show on top or top-thread loops show below, this is usually a tension issue. The correct tension for denim is around 4.5 on most sewing machines.

- If loops show on top, the issue is usually with the bobbin tension. If loops are showing on the bottom, the upper-thread tension may need adjusting.

- Pull on both threads to see if either feels stiff or loose; they should feel similar. Adjust the upper-thread tension using the dial on the machine. The bobbin tension is usually adjusted with a screw. Check your machine manual and tighten or loosen accordingly.

- If your stitches are looping and adjusting tension is not helping, your machine may need some oil.

DEALING WITH THICKNESSES

A jeans hem has four layers of denim and up to nine at the side seam. When a sewing machine struggles to sew through thick seams it's not always because the needle cannot pierce multiple layers. More often it just doesn't like the unevenness. When the machine hits a bump it causes the foot to tilt. This reduces the grip of the feed dog on the fabric and causes it to get jammed. A bulky seam aid or hump jumper can help to create a platform to even out the thickness. Place it butting up to the back of the sewing machine foot where you come across a particularly uneven section, like a seam.

Firmly pressing any thick seams with a steam iron before sewing can also help to reduce bumps and ease stitching. On very thick denims you can also give the bumps a bash with a hammer to flatten them out.

A PROFESSIONAL FINISH

My favourite piece of kit in our studio is the industrial steam iron. It's a game changer when sewing denim and the one thing I couldn't be without. While that's an unrealistic studio goal for most home sewers, the importance of good pressing cannot be overstated! For that reason I'd recommend investing in the best steam iron you can afford. Press each seam open as you sew, even if the seam will be pressed to the side later. Don't be tempted to leave all the pressing until the end. You can never achieve that sharp professional finish once all the seams have been assembled.

SEWING WITH STRETCH

Most jeans today contain stretch. On one hand this can make them softer and easier for domestic machines to handle, but stretch denim has its own sewing challenges.

To avoid wavy, puckered seams you will need to handle the fabric carefully and follow these tips.

- Clip or baste your seams together before sewing. Pinning is more likely to stretch the fabric.

- Avoid pulling or pushing the fabric through the machine; let it feed through naturally. If your machine has the option to reduce the pressure on the foot, this will help.

- Use a long stitch, 3.5–4 length.

- If joining fabrics from different jeans in an upcycling or patchwork project, choose fabrics of similar weight and elasticity. Be sure to cut pieces on the same grain line. The vast majority of jeans stretch only in the horizontal direction.

- Unless you are topstitching, stretch denim is best sewn with a 90/14 needle and multi-purpose thread. When topstitching it's advisable to use the thicker thread only on the top and normal multi-purpose thread on the bobbin.

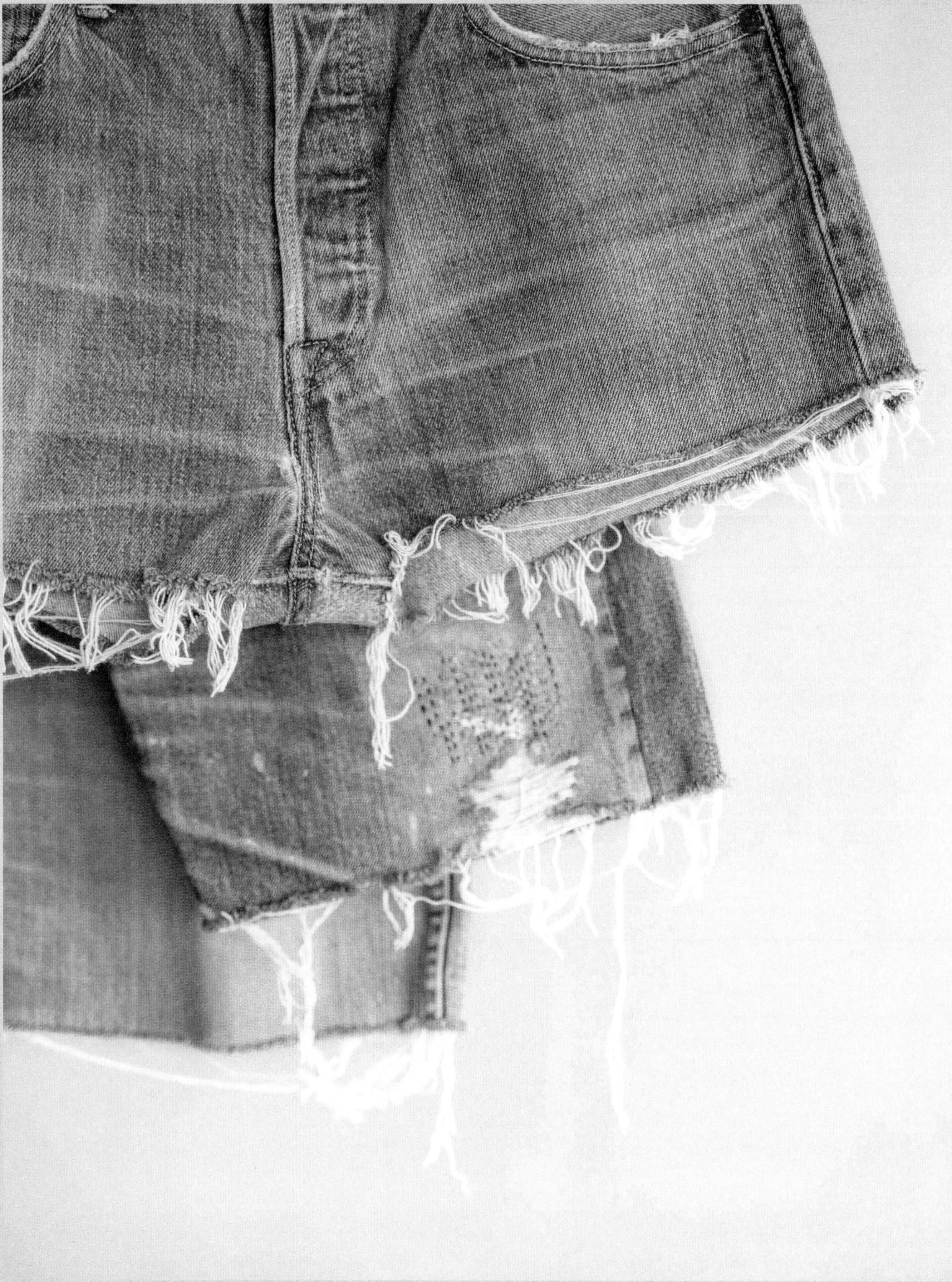

FRAYING AND DISTRESSING DENIM LIKE A PRO

It's totally fine to leave the cut edges of your shorts raw – they will naturally fray with time and washing, giving them a cool, lived-in look. But, if you're after something a bit more rugged, you can add texture with a little DIY distressing.

FRAYING THE HEMS

For that fluffy, fringed edge, gently pull out the horizontal threads (the white weft in typical indigo denim). Just tease them out bit by bit until you've got the level of fray you want. Feel free to leave the white threads hanging for a casual look, or trim them back if you're after a cleaner finish – it's like giving your shorts a haircut!

ADDING DISTRESSED HOLES

I wouldn't recommend adding rips to new denim. Besides being wasteful, creating those iconic, frayed holes is best done on worn jeans that are already softened up and wearing thin. A scalpel or even some fine sandpaper can be used to speed up the process. Scrape the surface, carefully breaking just the vertical warp threads and leaving the horizontal weft intact. Remove fluff as you go. Repeat until you're left with those classic white-threaded rips that add a bit of edge to your look.

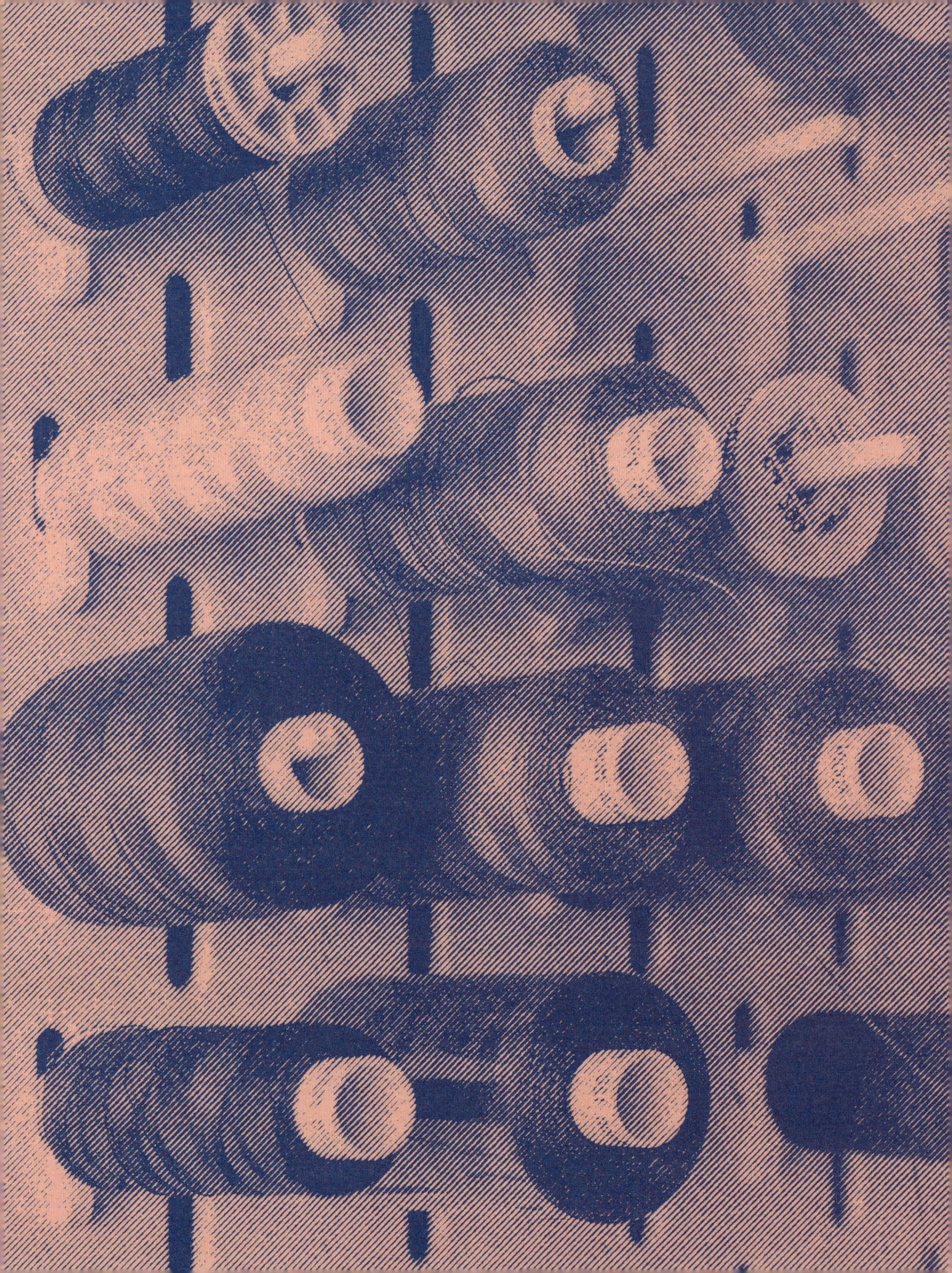

REPAIR

Are you sitting on a pile of worn-out denim? With a little time and some simple techniques, you can breathe new life into those old jeans. Set aside an evening at the sewing machine, or settle on the couch with some hand stitching while your favourite show plays in the background. Mending doesn't have to be a chore – it's a quiet, satisfying way to reconnect with your clothes, give them a second chance and keep them out of landfill.

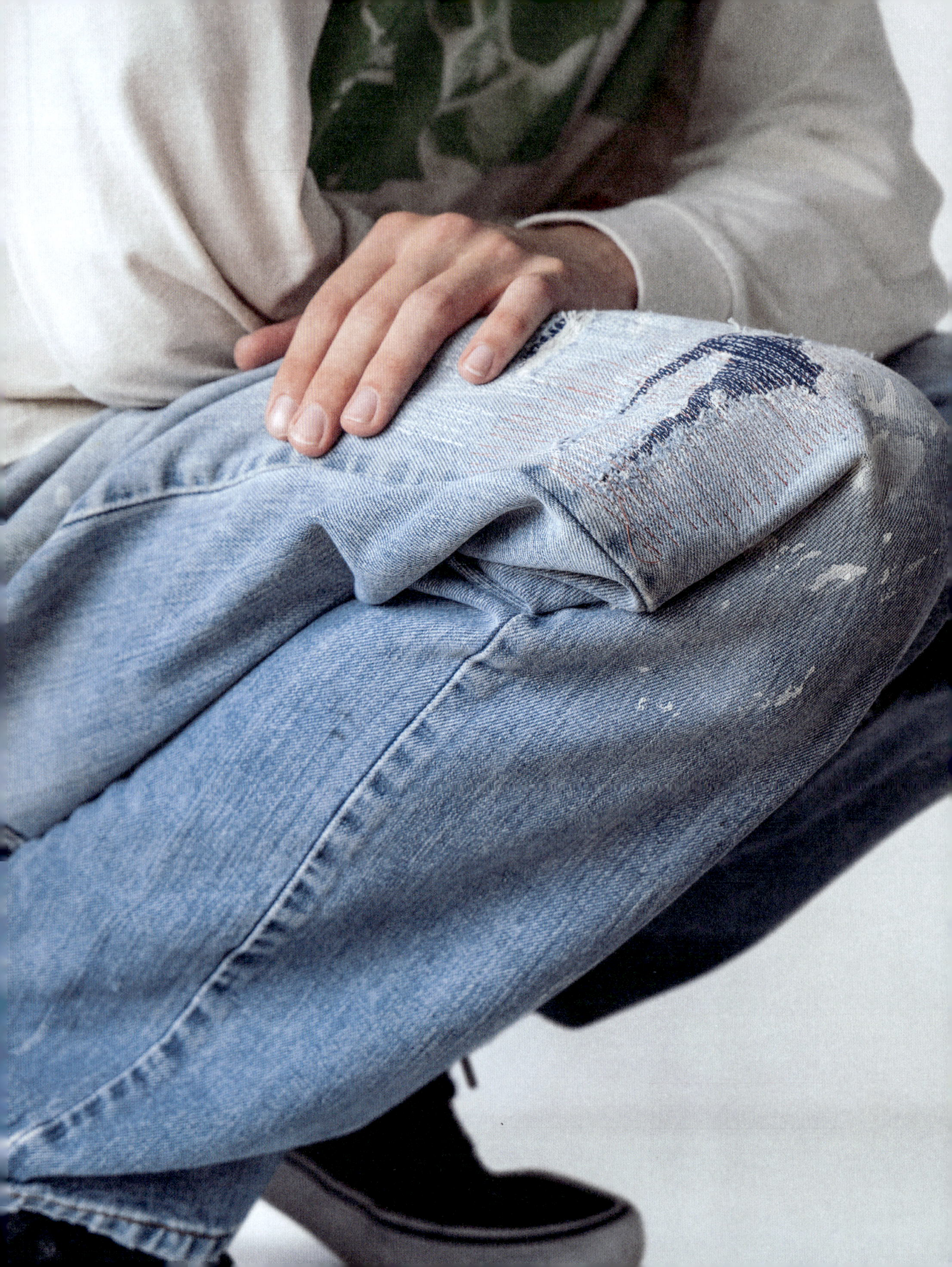

DARNING

A popular repair for jeans is darning, a technique that seamlessly restores rips and tears in your favourite denim pieces. In the studio, we rely on an industrial darning machine to perform this repair. The results are impressive but, weighing in at about 60kg (about 130lb), this beast of a machine is expensive and cumbersome. The great news is that, with a little patience and care, a perfectly decent mend can be achieved on any domestic sewing machine.

In this section, you'll learn how to robustly repair rips and common wear points on your jeans. I'll share insights from my professional experience that will ensure your repair is not only subtle but also strong. Some parts of your jeans can be difficult to reach on a sewing machine so I'll explain where to open seams for easier access. Once mastered, I've found darning to be a meditative and therapeutic process. As you mindfully weave your stitches, I hope you'll unlock a similar satisfaction from restoring something tired and broken to its former glory.

VISIBLE VS INVISIBLE

It's entirely up to you whether you want a bold repair or something more discreet. If you're looking for an invisible mend, choose threads and backing fabric to match your jeans. If you can't find an exact match, it's wise to go slightly lighter as denim fades over time but the thread will not. If you're up for something more distinctive, try experimenting with different thread colours and backing combos.

BASIC MACHINE-DARNING TECHNIQUE

YOU WILL NEED

- Denim scraps to use for backing the darned area
- Fabric shears
- Thread snips
- Pins or sewing clips
- Sewing machine
- All-purpose threads
- Steam iron
- Darning foot (optional)

Whether darning by hand or machine, the principle is essentially the same. Worn areas are replaced with careful lines of stitching. The methods we'll share here also use a patch to reinforce the fabric and create a base for the stitches.

TIPS FOR SUCCESS

- Always wash your garment first to allow holes that have stretched to return to their proper shape – especially important for knee and bum rips.

- Repair all the weakened fabric, not just the rip.

- Get in there quick at the first sign of a hole to reinforce the area before the rip appears.

- Don't choose a patch that's heavier than the garment you are mending.

- Never overlock or hem your patch. It may look a little untidy on the inside but a raw edge is softer and will help to avoid holes appearing around the patch.

- Never close up a hole by seaming the edges together like a scar as this will cause puckering. Instead, allow the fabric to relax and darn on top.

1 Inspect the area you are about to mend. Check for weakened fabric around the rip – this could look like pilling or thinning. It's important to reinforce all the weakened area because if you mend only the hole, the repair will soon fail around the edges. Cut a patch from the backing fabric to fit the area identified for mending.

2 Pin it to the inside of the garment using as few pins as possible around the edges. If you are mending a hole that is quite open, allow it to relax to its natural position – never stretch it open or pinch it closed. Transfer the pins one by one to the outside so you can easily remove them as you stitch.

3 Start stitching over the hole, forwards and backwards, using the reverse function on your machine and with a running stitch length of 2–3. For large areas, darn in small sections around 6cm (2⅜in) deep as reverse stitching can become difficult to control on larger areas.

4 If there is lots of excess fabric on the backing patch, trim it down to 5mm (³⁄₁₆in) around the darned area. Cut off any loose threads and press. If there are corners on the backing patch, round them off with scissors.

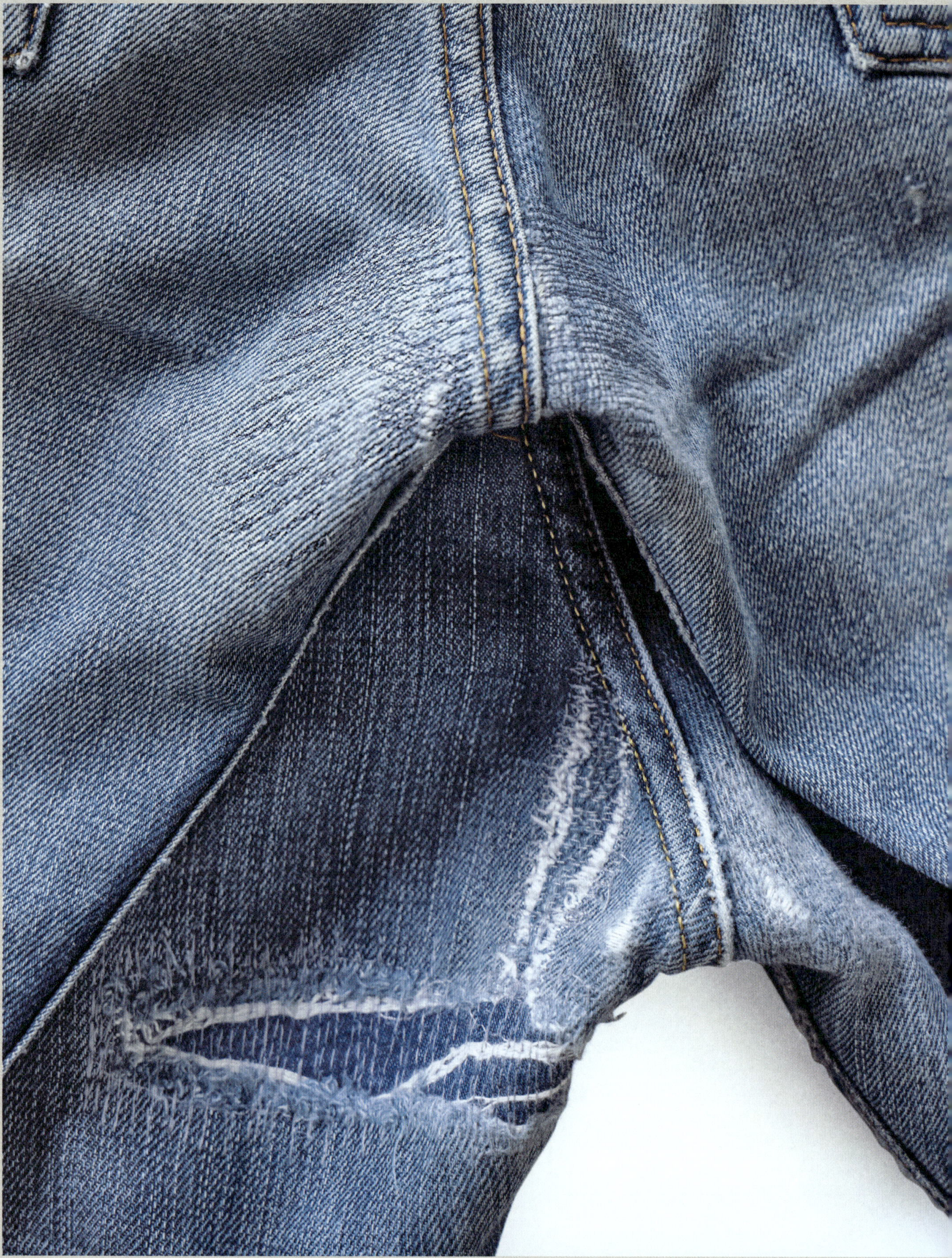

DARNING A CROTCH

The most common denim casualty of all is the classic crotch 'blowout.' It's indiscriminate – even the finest-quality jeans can wear out at the crotch long before their time. This awkward area can be daunting to repair, and we often see DIY fixes that, despite valiant efforts, don't hold up for long. Given that most of the jeans we see in recycling centres are discarded due to this problem, I'm on a mission to normalize the look of a repaired crotch and demystify the simple technique used to fix this annoying problem yourself.

You can tackle a worn-out or ripped crotch using the machine darning technique shown on pages 48–9. The following tips will help you to adapt that process to the crotch area.

DARN IN SMALL SECTIONS
The curvature of the rise can make it hard to get your garment to lie flat. If that's the case, darn in small sections, cutting loose and repositioning your garment when you need to so that you can darn more comfortably.

GO WIDE
Make sure the repair covers all of the worn area. Crotch repairs often fail because the repair was too small and the weakened area around the hole soon gives way.

POSITIONING YOUR JEANS
You can access the crotch by fully opening the fly. It won't be possible to get the whole crotch to lie flat but that's OK.

SUPPORT THE SEAM
If there is a hole or heavy wear very close to the seam, your patch will need to extend across the seam and be anchored on the other side. This has the dual benefit of reinforcing both sides of your crotch and stopping your repair from ripping next to the seam. With your jeans inside out, place a patch across the back rise and secure with a few pins. Darn on both sides of the centre back – as close as you can get to the seam. This can be done on any sewing machine.

> If you have a drop-feed setting on your machine, you can also switch to a darning foot and do a freehand darn in the same way.

DARNING RIPPED LEGS AND KNEES

I love a rockstar ripped jean but there's also a time and a place for a carefully mended knee and doing so will prolong the life of your garment. Perhaps you're a manual worker who finds their jeans wear out very quickly or you bought a pair of pre-ripped jeans and regretted it later. The leg and knee area can be awkward to darn as it's tricky to access with a sewing machine. Many of my customers avoid attempting a home repair for this reason but, once you get the hang of it, it's a quick and easy project.

1 Open the seam to access the rip – unless the damage is close to the top of the leg, in which case you can access it via the waist. It is usually easiest to open the side seam but if it's a felled seam or if it has topstitching, try opening the inside leg seam instead (see page 35 for how to open seams). As a rough guide, your opening should extend 5cm (2in) above and below your repair. Be sure to stop your seam ripper at least 4cm (1½in) clear of the hip bar tack and hem as this will make it easier to close the seam back up.

2 Cut a patch to place over the back of your repair and pin it in place. Remember to check the surrounding area for weakness and plan your repair to reinforce where needed. Sometimes it's necessary for the inner patch to cover almost the entire thigh. Whether the patch is big or small, I would always recommend extending it into the side seam. You are now ready to darn the area using the machine-darning technique on page 48–9. Place the jeans on the sewing machine, using the open side seam to ensure that the back panel is out of the way and you don't accidentally stitch through it.

3 When you have finished darning, close up the side seam with a running stitch. If there was overlocking on the seam allowance, replace it or do a wide zigzag stitch. If your repair has caused the knee to bulge and the side seam is no longer straight (this can happen particularly on stretch denim), stitch in a straight line. Do not follow the bulge.

STITCH DIRECTION AND TENSION FOR DARNING

This can be a personal decision but I like to stitch as follows for these repairs:

Leg and knee repairs: darn in a vertical direction.

Slashes and small holes: an invisible darn with quite dense stitching.

Large open holes and on very stretchy denim: go for more open stitching to allow the fabric to be able to stretch a little.

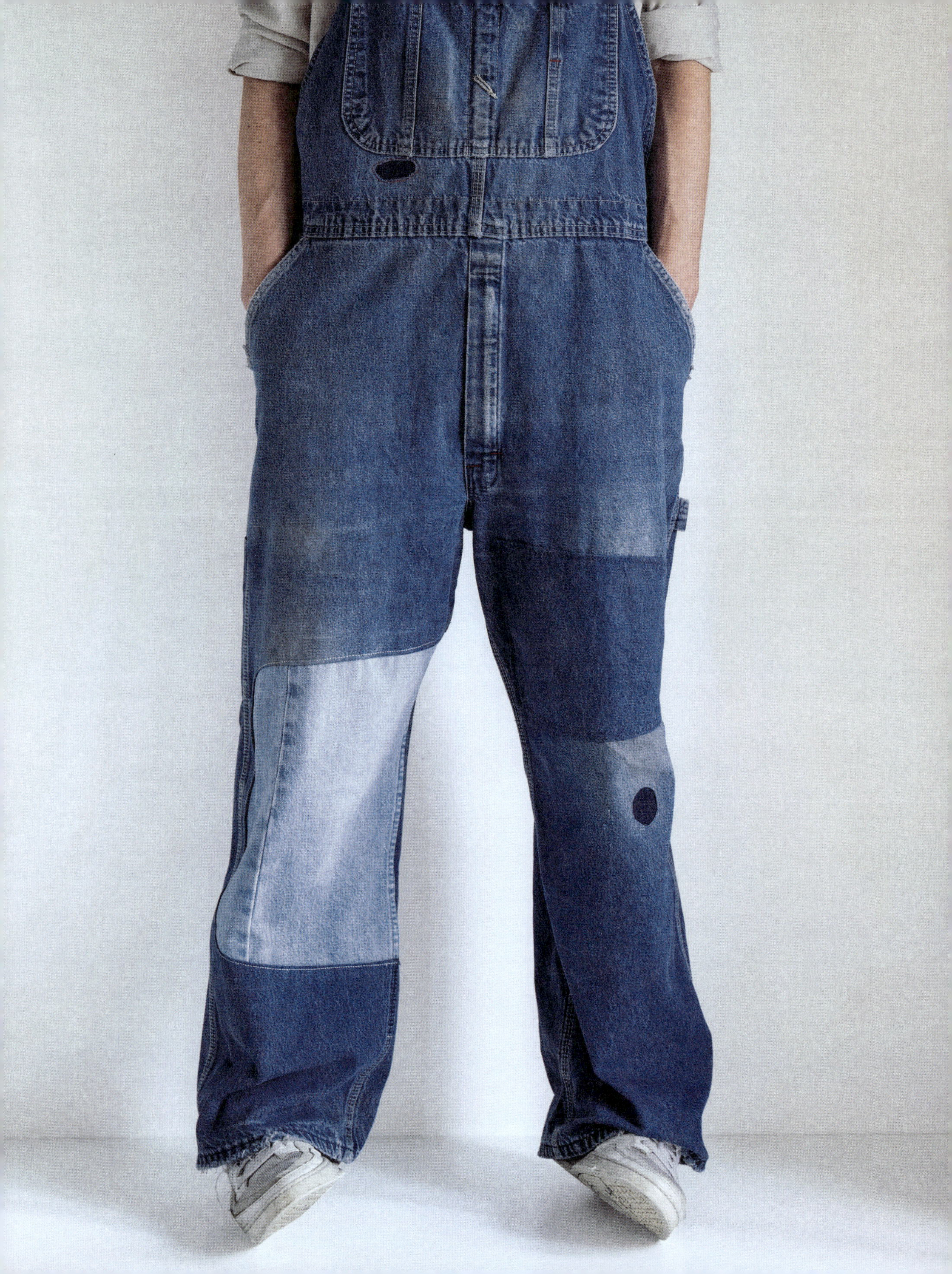

PATCHING

YOU WILL NEED

- Denim scraps in a weight and elasticity similar to your garment
- Tailor's chalk or fabric marker
- Ruler
- Pencil and paper
- Pins or sewing clips
- Seam ripper
- Fabric shears
- Thread snips
- Scalpel
- Heavy-duty topstitch threads
- Sewing machine
- Denim sewing-machine needles
- Steam iron

In this section we'll explain how to patch up rips using a sewing machine. It's a straightforward mend that adds character to your jeans. The patches can be as bold or as subtle as you like. I love to experiment with shade and texture, choosing denim with interesting fade and weave effects.

This tutorial walks you through adding patches on the front of jeans or dungarees to cover a hole, or on the back to make a feature of the rip. You can easily adapt the technique to other denim garments.

TIPS TO MAKE YOUR PATCHES LOOK GREAT

- Go for a fabric that's similar in weight to your jeans – it will sit better.
- If you're working with stretch denim, make sure your patch has a similar elasticity and be sure to cut it with the grain line matching your jeans. This helps avoid any weird puckering after washing.

FRONT PATCH METHOD

1 Mark the size of the patch you need onto the jeans using chalk.

2 Measure and then draw the patch onto a piece of paper, adding a 1cm (⅜in) seam allowance to the top, bottom and inside edges. Cut it out. You can leave the outside edge a little wider than your jeans at this point to be trimmed down later.

3 Using a seam ripper, open the side seam of the jeans, making sure to stop around 4cm (1½in) below the hip bar tack and 4cm (1½in) above the hem. The opening should extend roughly 5cm (2in) above and below your patch. If your jeans have a fully felled side seam it will be difficult to open and close it up nicely. You can still patch your jeans using this method but instead of opening the side seam, open the inside leg seam and follow the same steps.

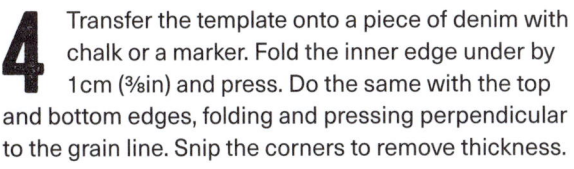

4 Transfer the template onto a piece of denim with chalk or a marker. Fold the inner edge under by 1cm (⅜in) and press. Do the same with the top and bottom edges, folding and pressing perpendicular to the grain line. Snip the corners to remove thickness.

5 Pin the patch in position over the area to be mended on the front of the jeans and edge stitch around three sides leaving the side adjacent to the seam. Stitch 2mm (¹⁄₁₆in) from the edge using a straight stitch, topstitch thread and a denim needle.

6 Trim off the overhanging part of the patch that is next to the side seam edge to match to the width of the front panel including the side seam allowance.

7 Turn the jeans inside out and stitch the opened part of the side seam closed using a sewing machine, then press. Finish the edges of the seam allowance with zigzag stitching or overlocking. If your jeans have an open-seam construction you should do this before closing up the seam.

FULL-PANEL REPLACEMENT
This is just a very large patch cut from the leg of a donor jean. This method is ideal for jeans where the whole front panel is wearing thin. You can lay it on top using the patch method, but I like to attach it at the back with a turned-in edge. The technique is the same as the Reverse Patch on page 62 – it's just a much bigger patch! Be sure to replace all the thinning fabric; don't worry if the panel ends up quite big.

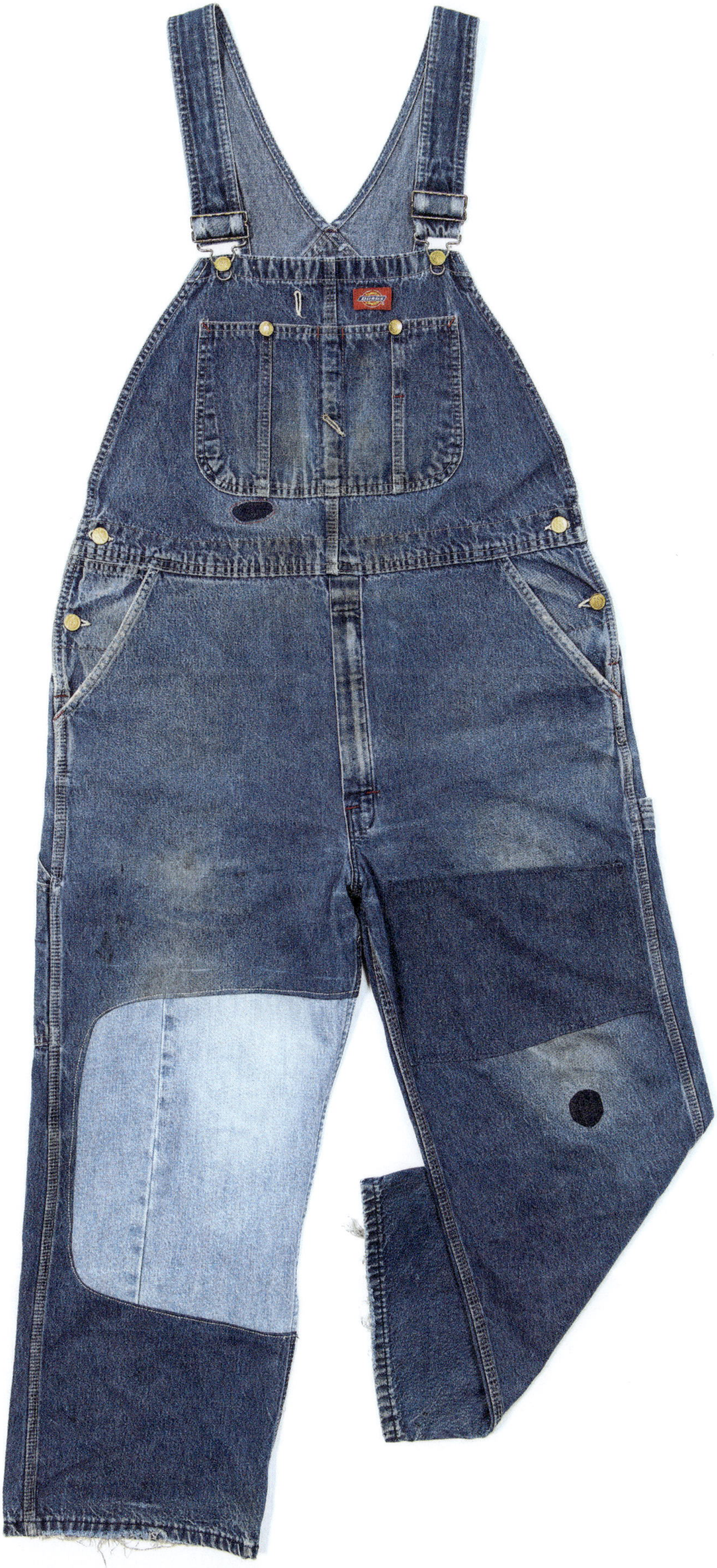

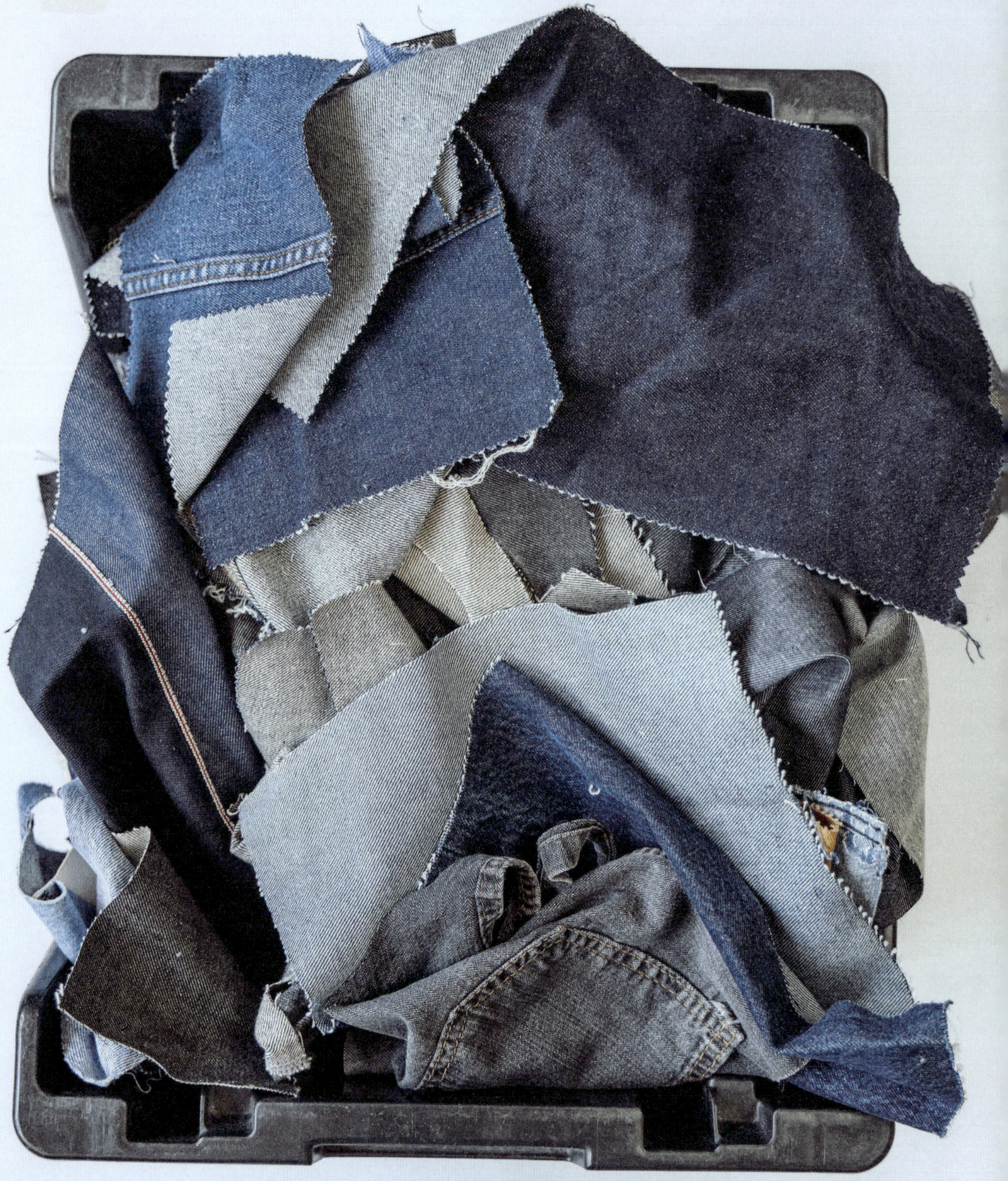

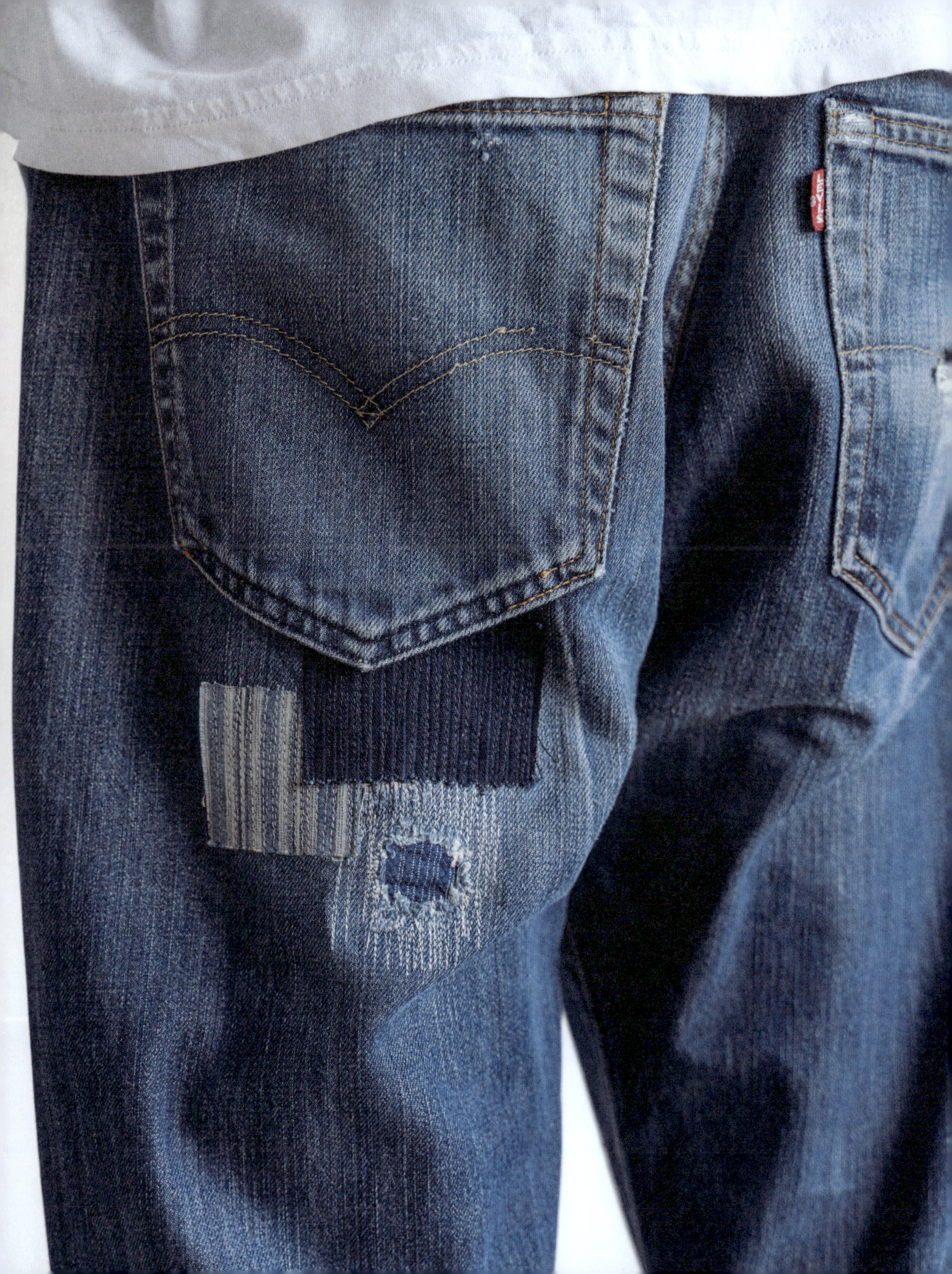

REVERSE PATCH METHOD

To add a patch behind the rip, use the same process as for the front patch method on page 56 but with a few adjustments.

1 Turn the garment inside out and mark the area to patch with a fabric pen or tailor's chalk. Turn the garment back to the right side out. Fold and press the edges of the patch towards the right side of the patch. The right side of the patch should be showing through.

2 Have a think about whether you want to have a raw edge or a clean edge on the visible hole. If you want a clean edge, you should press the edges of the hole under. Topstitch around the perimeter of the hole.

3 Alternatively, if you want to keep the raw edge of the hole, stitch around the perimeter about 5mm (3/16in) from the edge. Or, you could loosely darn around the perimeter onto the patch.

IDEAS FOR ADDING MORE DETAIL

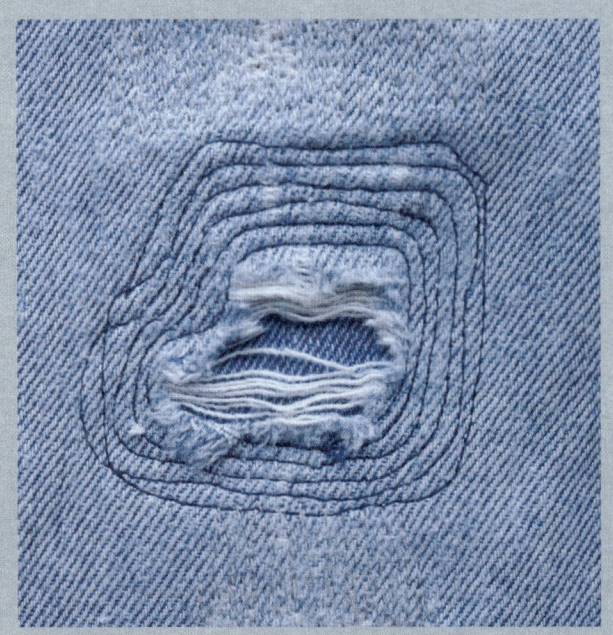

Play with topstitching.

Darn over the top of the patch.

Incorporate seam details.

Use dropped hem details on the edges.

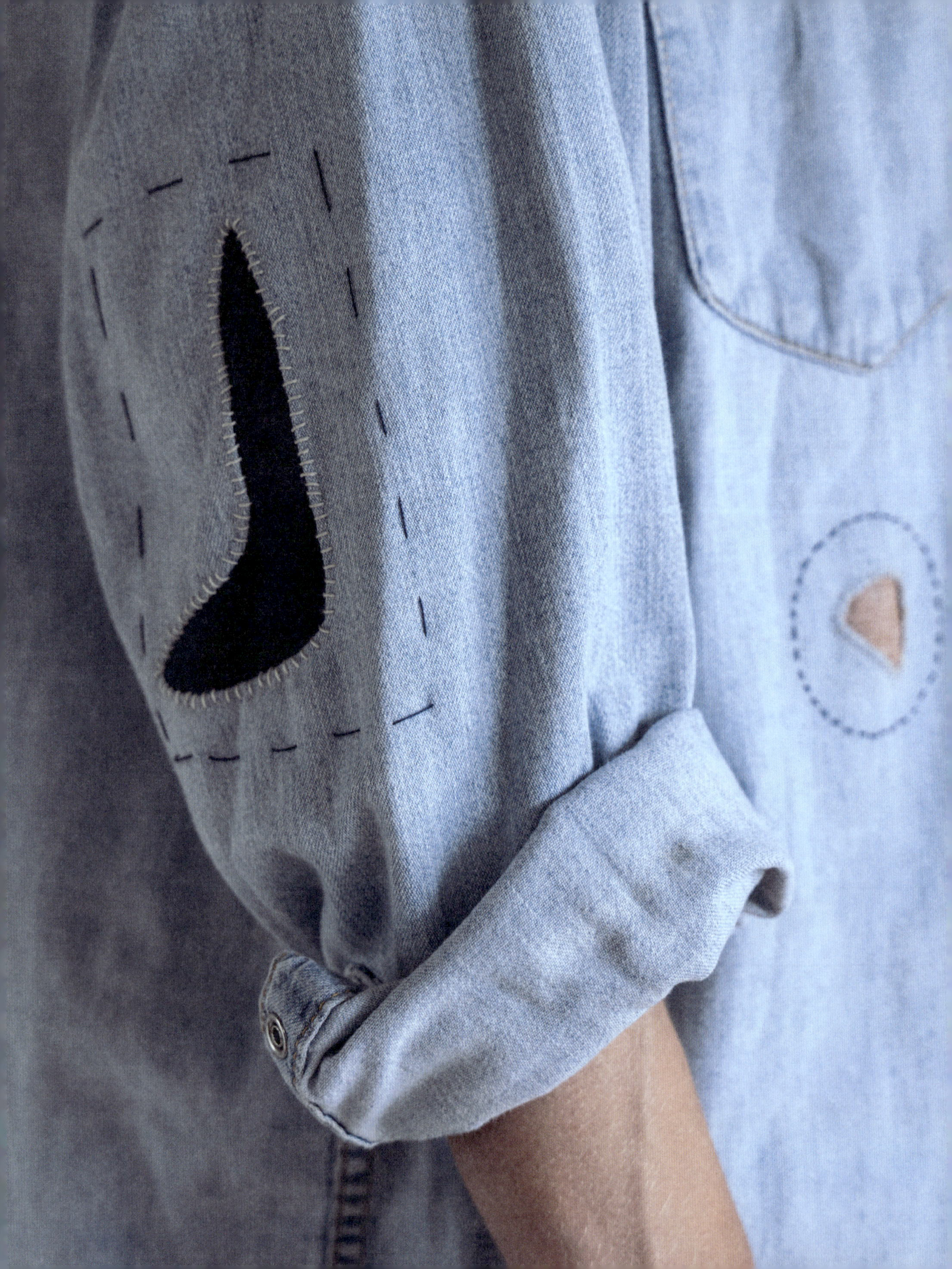

HAND-STITCHED REPAIRS

YOU WILL NEED

- ☐ Fabric scraps for patching
- Sashiko thread
- Sashiko needle (or long darning needle)
- Tailor's chalk or pencil
- Pins
- Darning hoop (optional)
- Thimble
- Steam iron

The delicate hand-stitching technique Sashiko, meaning 'small stab', originates in Japan, where it has been practised for centuries. Initially used to extend the life of clothing worn by peasant workers, Sashiko has gained widespread appeal. It is now a favoured mending technique, particularly for denim and modern workwear, thanks to its humble origins and the rich archive of Japanese indigo textiles. *Sashiko* can be both decorative and functional. While the most intricate patterns require time and practice to master, even the basic technique can produce stunning results and is totally achievable for a patient beginner.

THE STITCHES

WHIP STITCH

Thread a needle and knot the end. Insert the needle from the back of the fabric to the front at the outside edge of the top piece. Pull through, then insert the needle again near the first stitch, about 5mm (3/16in) away, and pull through. Repeat this process along the edge, forming a diagonal pattern with evenly spaced stitches. For a clean finish, tie a knot at the end of the last stitch and trim the excess thread.

BACKSTITCH

Bring the needle up from the back of the fabric to the front at your starting point (A). Push the needle back down through the fabric a short distance behind (B), making a short stitch, usually about 4mm (3/16in) long. Now bring the needle up again, this time a stitch length in front of your starting point (C) and repeat.

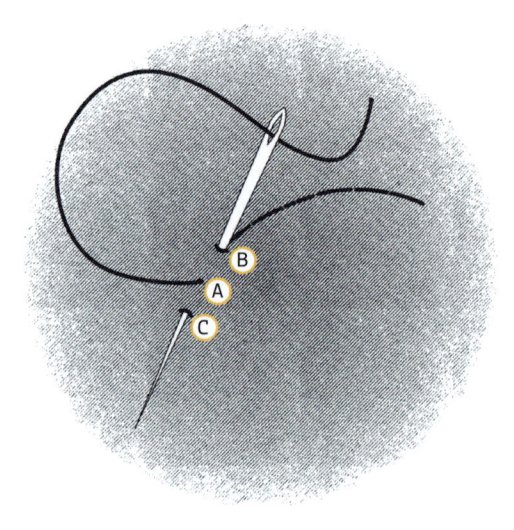

SASHIKO (OR RUNNING) STITCH

With the needle, stab in and out of the fabric, loading three or more stitches at a time onto the needle. Repeat as required keeping the stitches even in length and spacing.

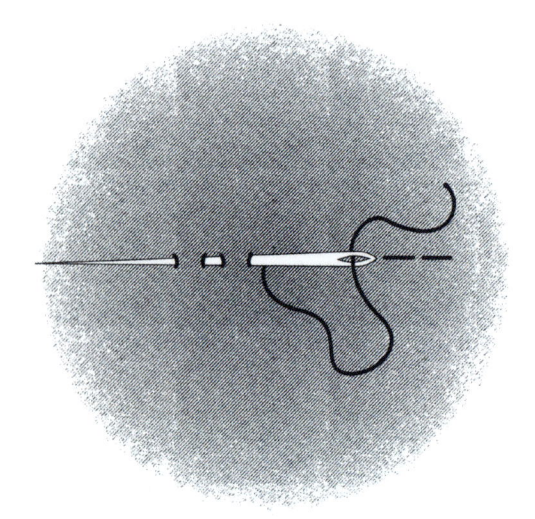

TACK STITCH

Just a long, quick running stitch used to temporarily attach pieces by simply passing the needle in then out in a forwards direction. Stitch length is usually 1cm (3/8in) or more and it doesn't have to be straight or evenly spaced.

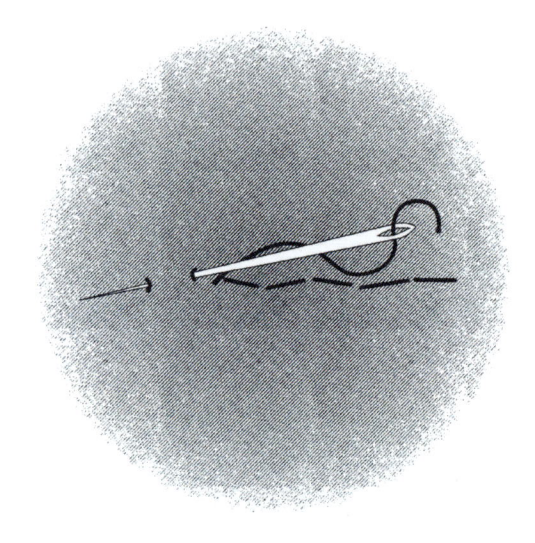

NEEDLES AND THREAD

While it's definitely possible to get started with a regular darning needle and embroidery threads, there are real advantages to acquiring some specialist kit. Sashiko needles are longer than normal darning needles, allowing you to load more stitches. They have a sharp point for piercing heavy fabrics and a wide eye for carrying thick thread.

Embroidery yarns tend to be made up of multiple twisted strands. This can cause them to get tangled when stitching dense materials. In contrast, Sashiko threads are made of a single twisted strand. They also use longer-staple cotton fibres, making them stronger. It's really worth investing in these basics if you're getting into mastering the process.

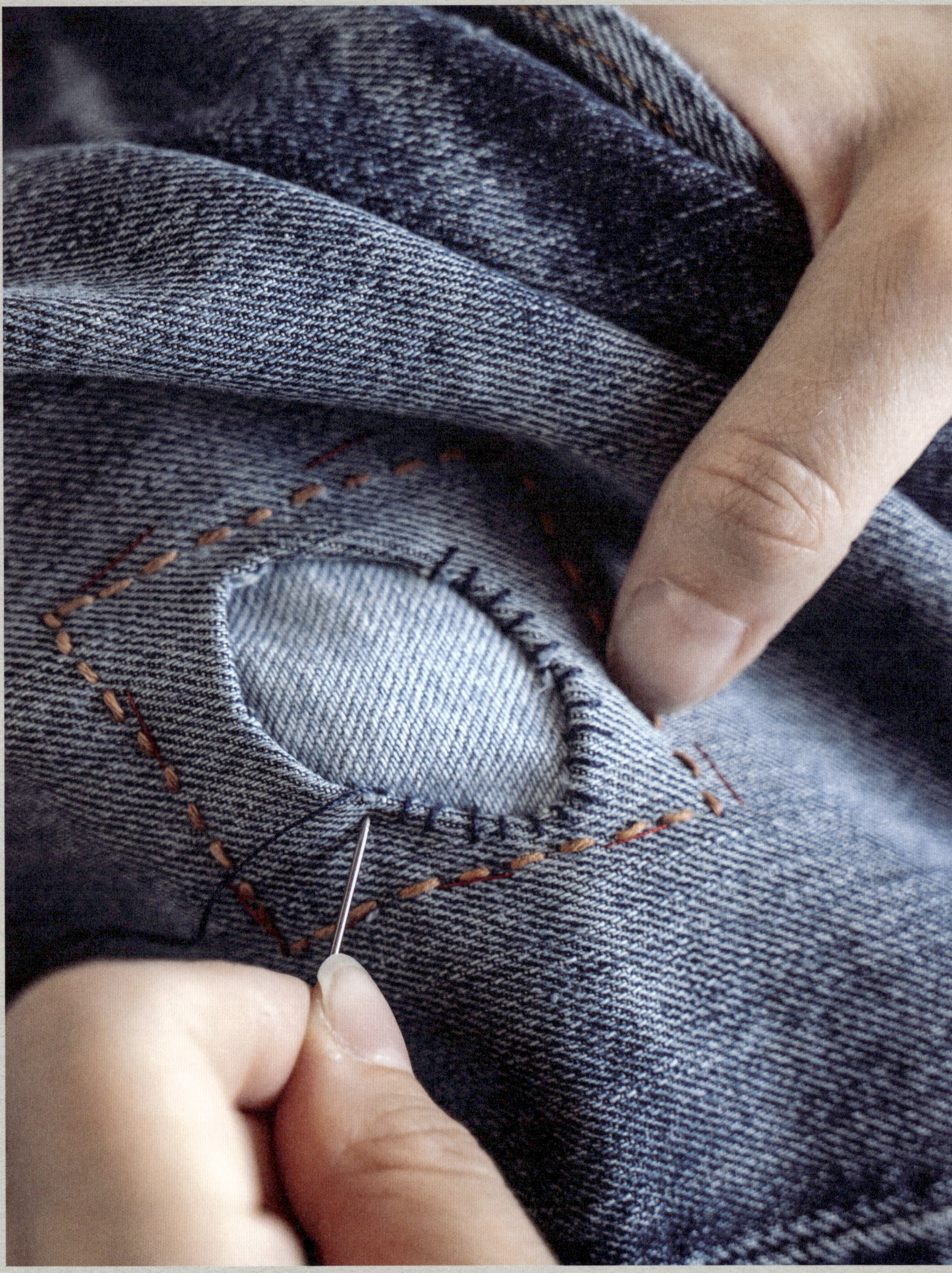

WHIP-STITCH PATCH

A quick and effective mending option, whip stitching the edges of your rip will prevent it from fraying further, while the patch behind should be big enough to reinforce weak areas around it.

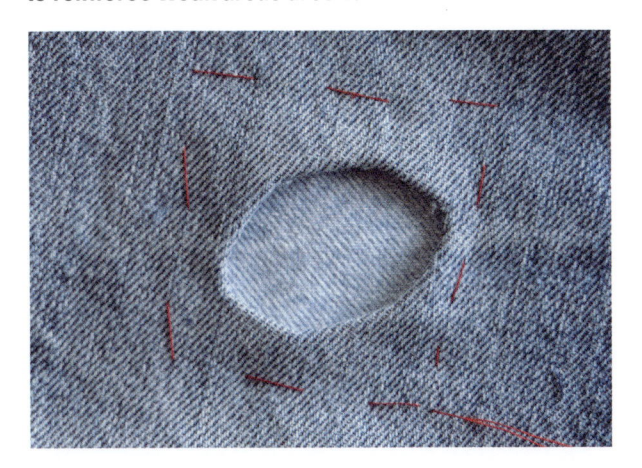

1 Mark and cut out a patch. I don't turn in the edges when hand-mending denim as the corners become difficult to sew through. Turn in the edges of the rip towards the inside of the garment and press. Pin the patch in place on the reverse of the jeans before tacking around the edge with a long stitch. Remove the pins.

2 Backstitch around the edges of the patch about 3mm (⅛in) from the edge. You should be able to feel the edge of the patch from the inside. At the end, push the needle to the back, tie a knot to secure the thread and trim any excess threads.

3 Whip stitch around the opening of the rip. When you've finished, push the needle to the back, tie a knot to secure the thread and trim any excess threads. Remove the tacking stitches.

SIMPLE SASHIKO PATCH (INSIDE)

1 Mark and cut a patch, similar in weight to the original fabric or slightly lighter.

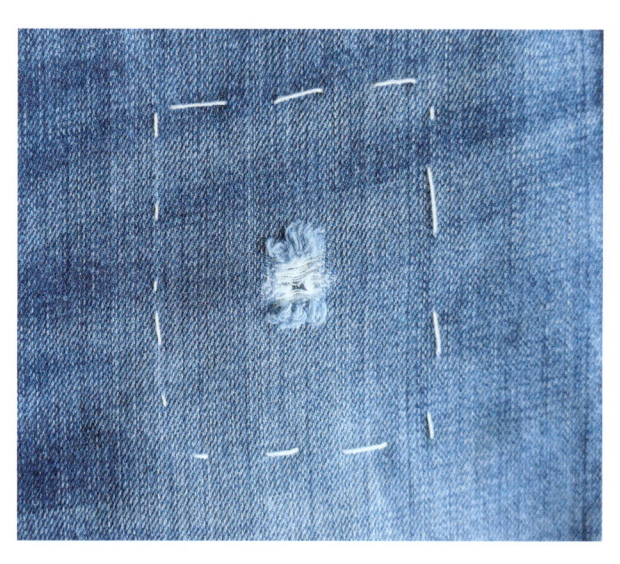

2 Pin the patch in place on the reverse of the denim. Tack around the edge of the patch to hold it in place and remove the pins.

3 With chalk or pencil, mark vertical stitch rows to fill the patch – your rows should be no more than 7mm (¼in) apart and the denser your *Sashiko* stitches are, the stronger your mend will be. If you have a keen eye, you can skip the marking stage and stitch your rows freehand.

4 Thread your needle with *Sashiko* thread and knot the end. Find the corner of your patch and pull the needle through from inside to outside. Begin stitching in rows of short running stitches, remembering that the desired effect is a small stab stitch. At the end of the row, push the needle inside, bring it out at the start of the next row and repeat.

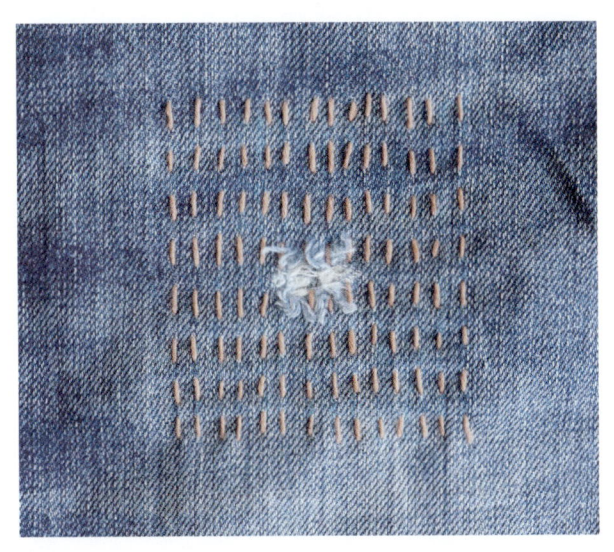

> You can add extra reinforcement around the rip by stitching additional lines in between the original rows. Alternatively, you could add horizontal stitches in this area that intersect the vertical stitches, creating little crosses.

5 Once you've covered the rip and reinforced the area, push the needle to the back, tie a knot to secure the thread and trim any excess threads. Remove the tacking stitches.

SASHIKO PATCH (OUTSIDE)

Whether to place your patch on the outside or the inside is an aesthetic choice; the technique is the same. Both have equal integrity as a repair, but if you have a particularly lovely scrap you want to use, you may choose to place it on the outside of your garment. For patching denim, I like to use indigo patterns but batik or utility fabrics such as navy twill and railroad stripes also work really well. But the truth is there are no rules and you can use whatever you have available. Just keep in mind that if your garment is made from a stretchy fabric you should look for something with similar elasticity and avoid patching it with rigid fabrics.

HAND-MENDING TIPS

All of these mends are entirely doable by hand but if you have a sewing machine you may prefer to open up the side seams for easier access to the area. See Step 3 on page 35.

You may find it helps to use an embroidery hoop – it depends on the position. I find it useful for lighter fabrics as they are easier to stitch when pulled taut.

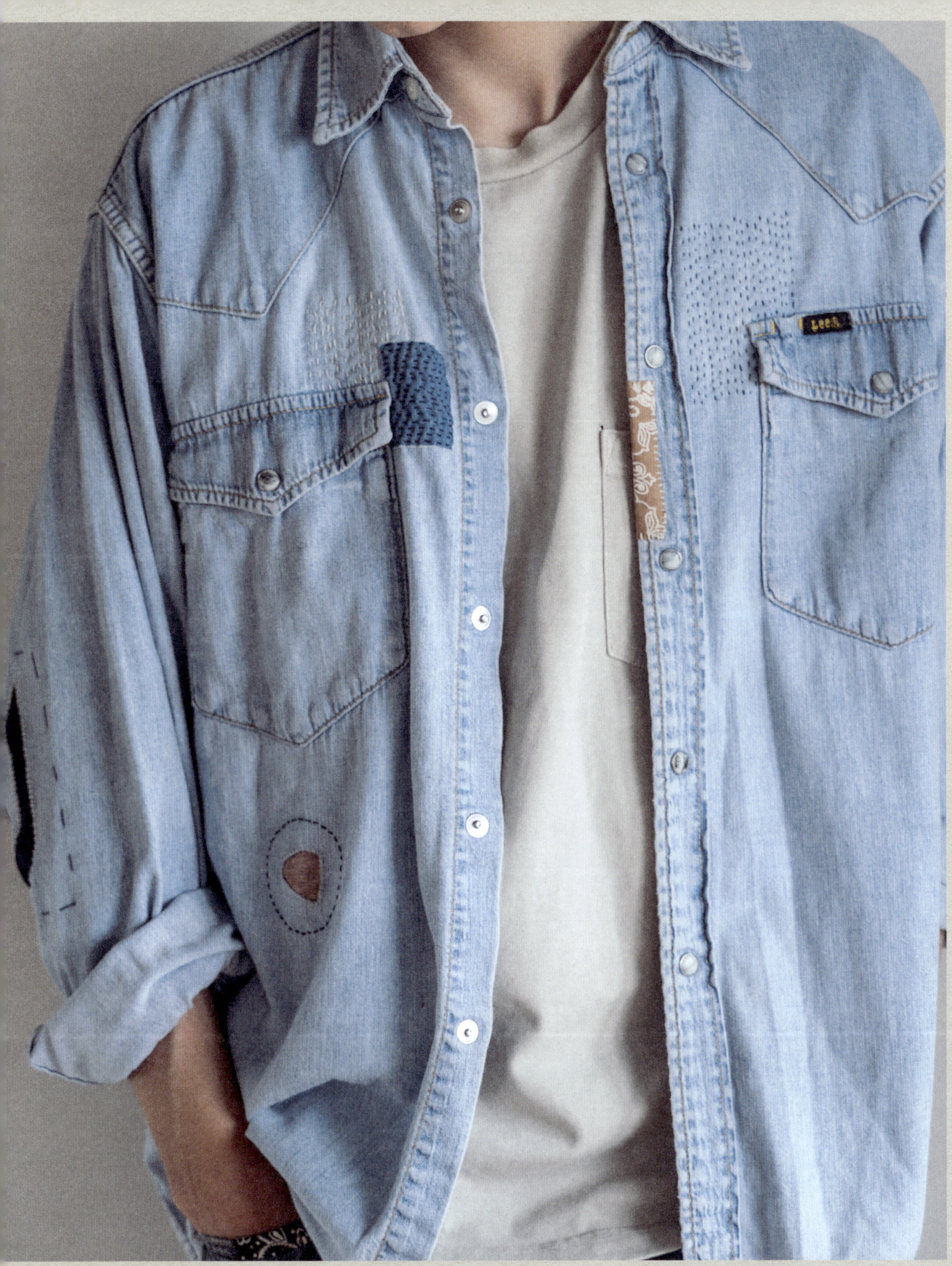
Lee

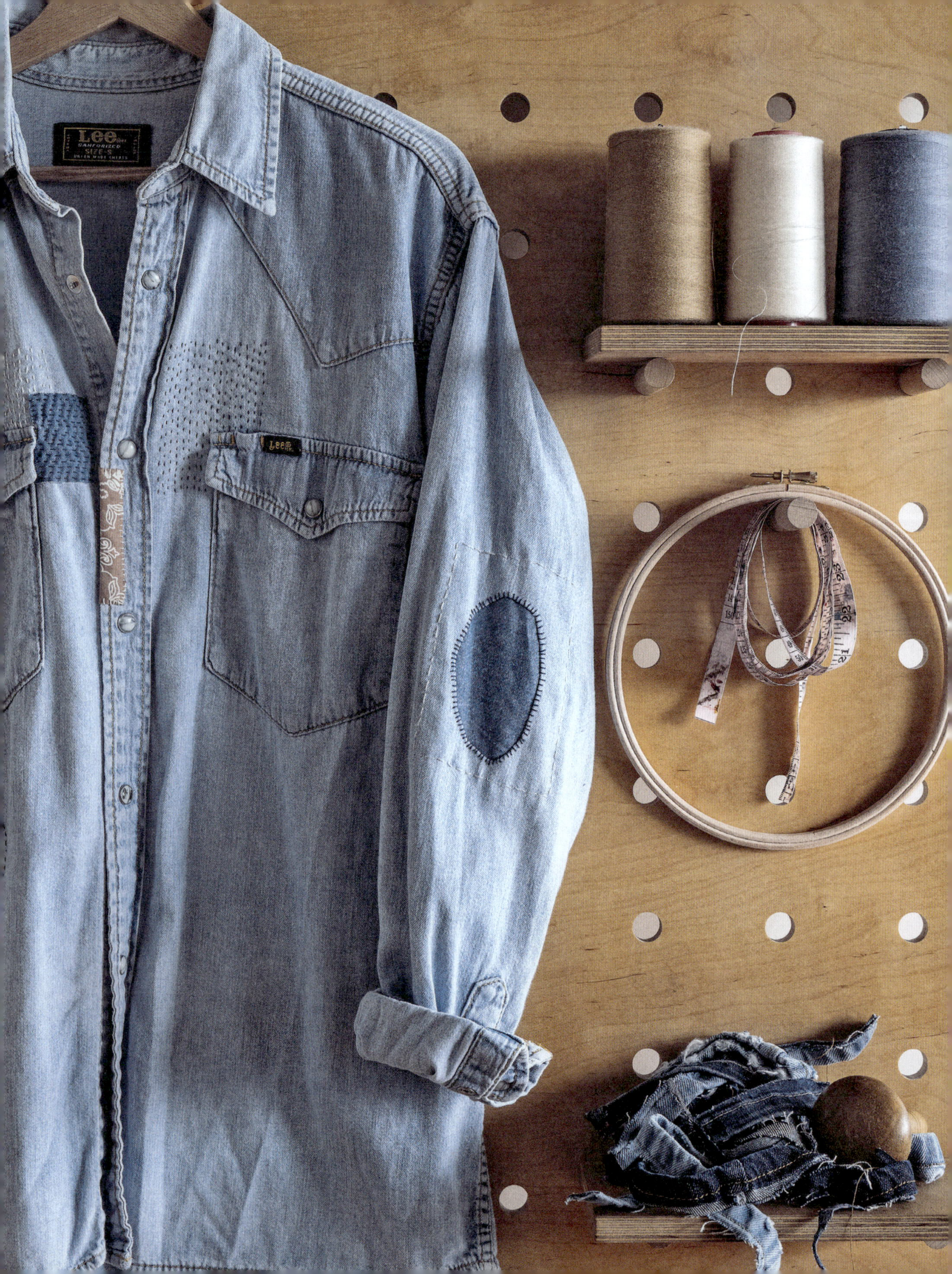
Lee
SANFORIZED
SIZE S
Lee

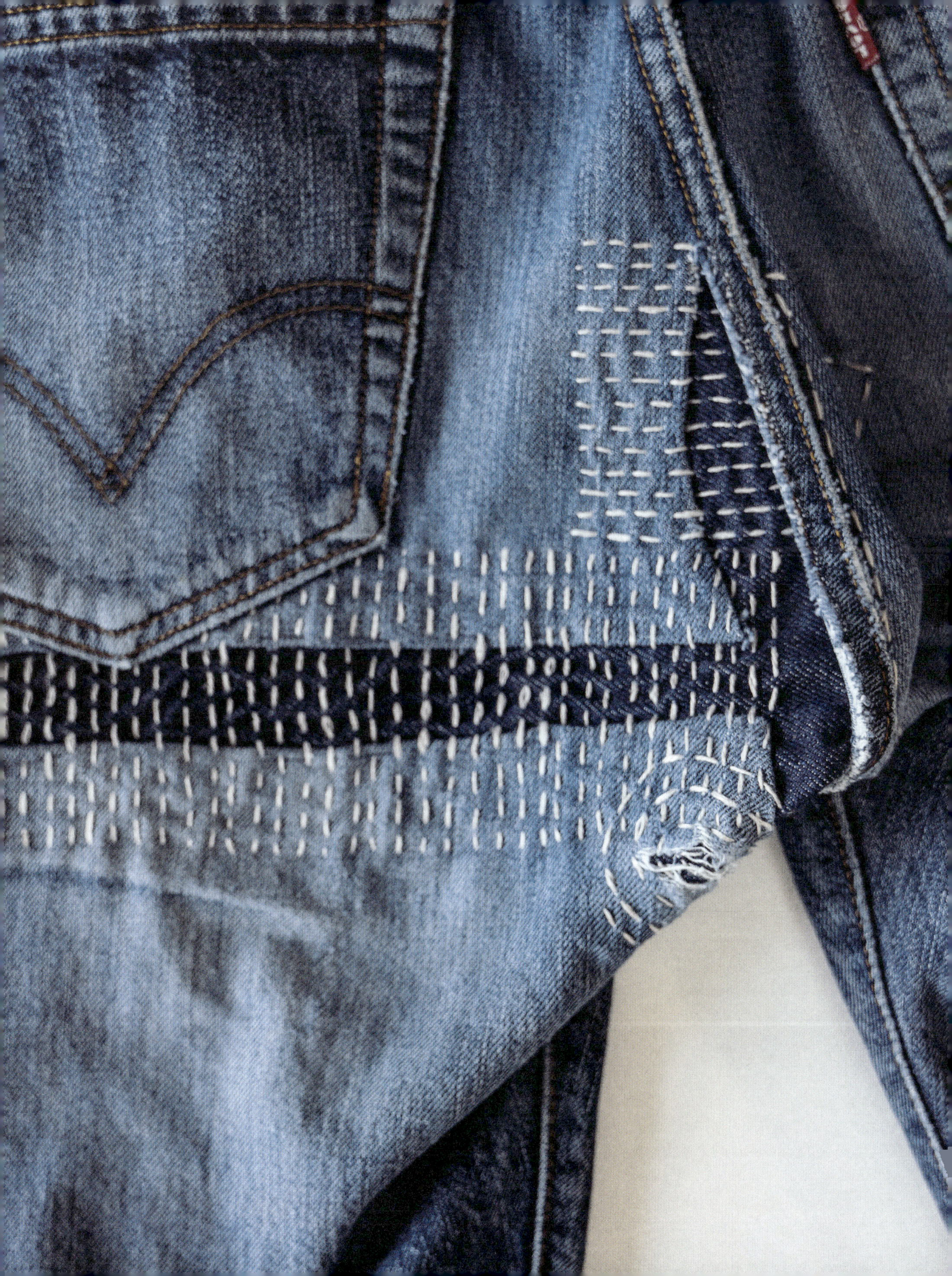

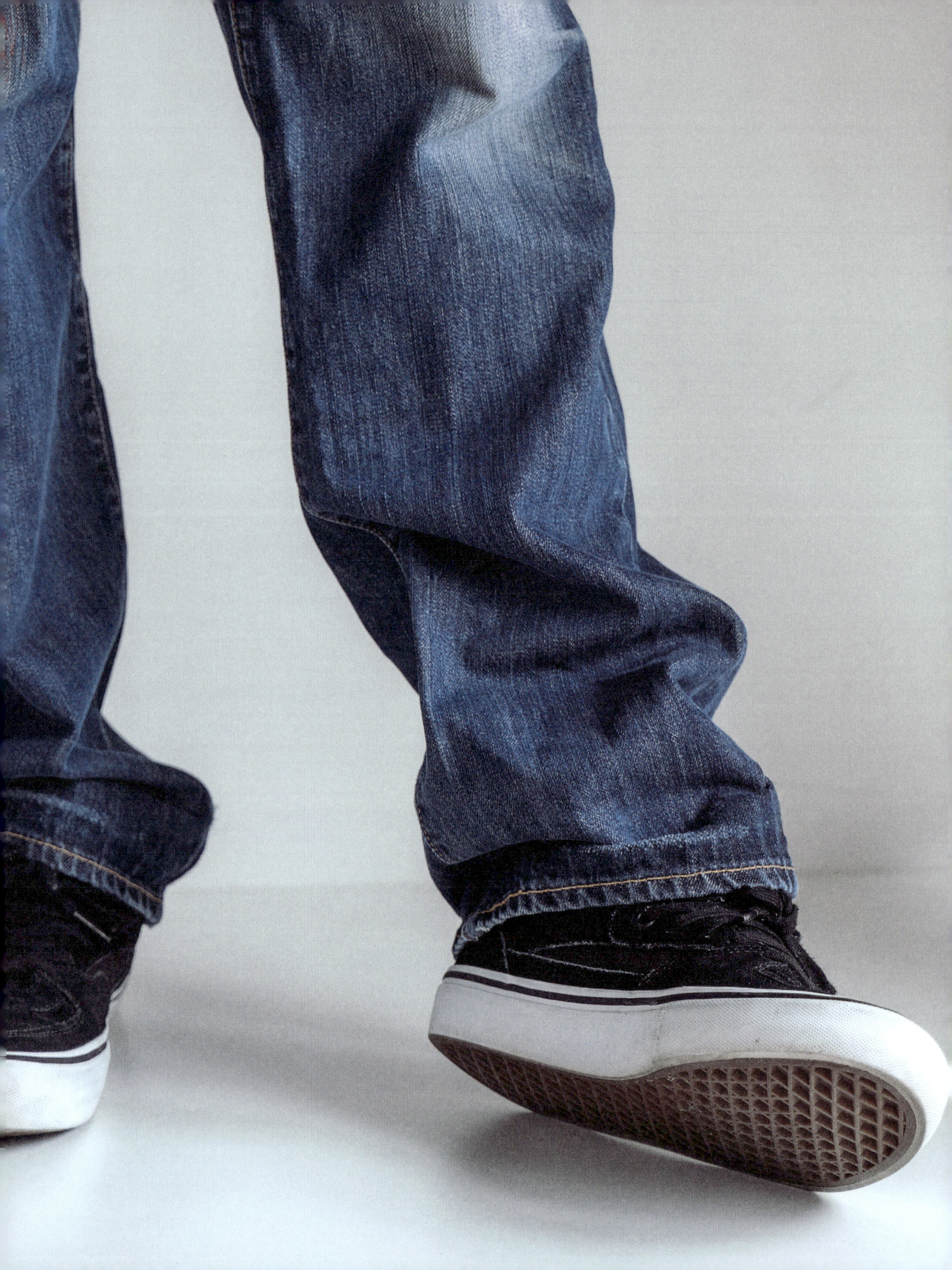

ALTERING HEMS

YOU WILL NEED

- Tape measure
- Tailor's chalk or fabric marker
- Pins or sewing clips
- Fabric shears
- Seam ripper
- Scalpel
- Heavy-duty topstitch threads
- All-purpose threads (matching your jeans)
- Sewing machine
- Denim sewing-machine needles
- Hump jumper
- Steam iron

This is a handy skill that anyone can learn. It differs from regular trouser hemming because of the thickness and details unique to denim fabric. In this section I'll show you two different techniques, classic and original hemming, and give you the confidence to shorten all sorts of denim.

MEASURING AND MARKING

FOR BOTH METHODS

Try on your jeans and decide what you would like the new length to be by turning the fabric under until you like how it looks. Remember to consider what sort of shoes you'd normally wear with the jeans and check the length with different footwear. When you're happy with the length, place a few pins to hold it in place, take the jeans off and measure the new inside leg seam length. Make a note of it.

CLASSIC HEMMING

With this method the jeans are shortened and hems resewn like-for-like. This is perfect for dark-coloured jeans where there's little or no fading. Jeans hems are very bulky on the side seams and you could be dealing with up to five layers of fabric, so a sturdy sewing machine is needed.

1 Turn the jeans inside out. Measure the inside leg seam length you require and mark with a line parallel to the original jeans hem. Add a 2.5cm (1in) seam allowance below this line and mark with chalk. If you are shortening by less than 3.5cm (1⅜in) you may need to open the hem stitching with a seam ripper.

2 Cut along the lower marked line, removing the original hem.

3 With the jeans still inside out, fold the bottom edge up by 1.5cm (½in) and press with an iron to create a crease. Fold up another 1.5cm (½in) to conceal the cut edge. Press firmly and secure the hem in place with clips.

> The bump on the side seam can be particularly challenging for domestic machines. You can use a bulky seam aid or 'hump jumper' to help (see page 27).

4 Turn the jeans the right way out. Using the denim needle and topstitching thread, set up your sewing machine with a stitch length matching the hem on your jeans. Test your set-up on the hem that you have cut off. Use a straight stitch to sew the hem, stitching just below your fold on the front side of the jeans. This should be 1cm (⅜in) from the edge but keep checking as you go that the stitches catch the hem.

5 The finished hem. Repeat for the other leg.

ORIGINAL HEMMING

This method involves cutting off the hem and reattaching it, almost invisibly, back onto your jeans. This has a number of benefits; if your jeans are vintage or have a vintage-look wash, it allows you to preserve the wear and tear on the hem. It's also a good alternative if your sewing machine struggles with thick seams.

1 Turn your jeans inside out. Measure the inside leg seam length you require and mark with a chalk line parallel to the original jeans hem (see step 1 on page 78). Measure the distance from the bottom of the original hem to the mark you made. This will be the amount you need to fold into your pleat. Turn the jeans back to the right side. Fold the hem up to the chalk line. Measure from the folded edge to the top of the original hem. This should be half the length of the first measurement. Pin this fold in place.

2 Sew a straight stitch as close as possible to the top edge of the original hem to secure the pleat. Press firmly.

3 When the jeans are turned back to the right side, the leg will be shortened by the amount of fabric sewn into the pleat sitting on the inside. Press firmly with lots of pressure and steam.

4 Trim off the excess fabric leaving 1cm (⅜in) seam allowance and finish the edge with overlocking or zigzag stitch. Repeat for the other leg.

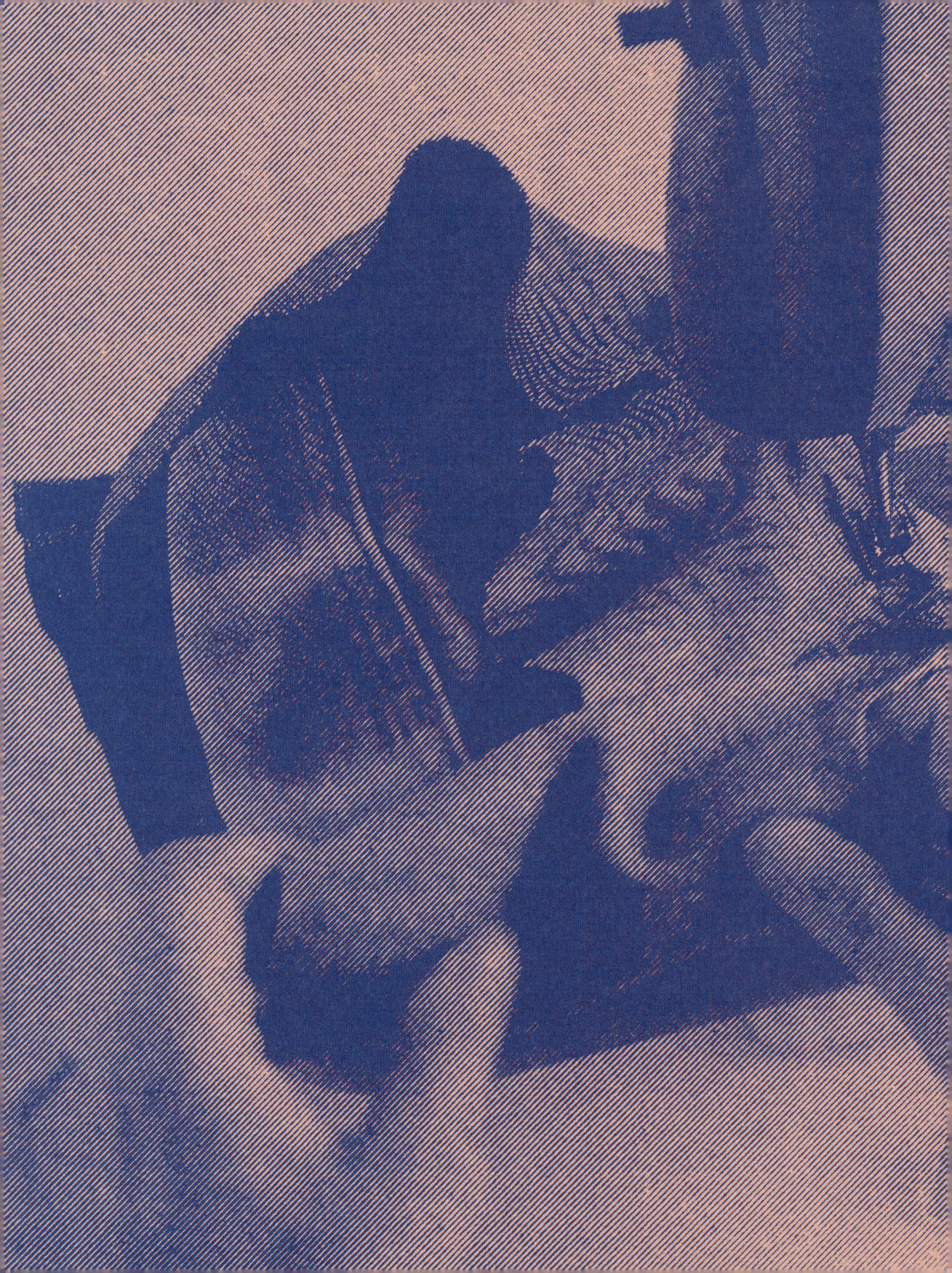

RESTYLE

In the time it takes to hit the shops and trawl for a new pair of jeans there's so much you can do with a pair that's already lurking unworn in your wardrobe. The tutorials in this chapter will give you confidence and buckets of inspiration to get creative with what you've got at your disposal. You'll save time, money, reduce your environmental footprint and look amazing. Perhaps you'll never buy a new pair of jeans again!

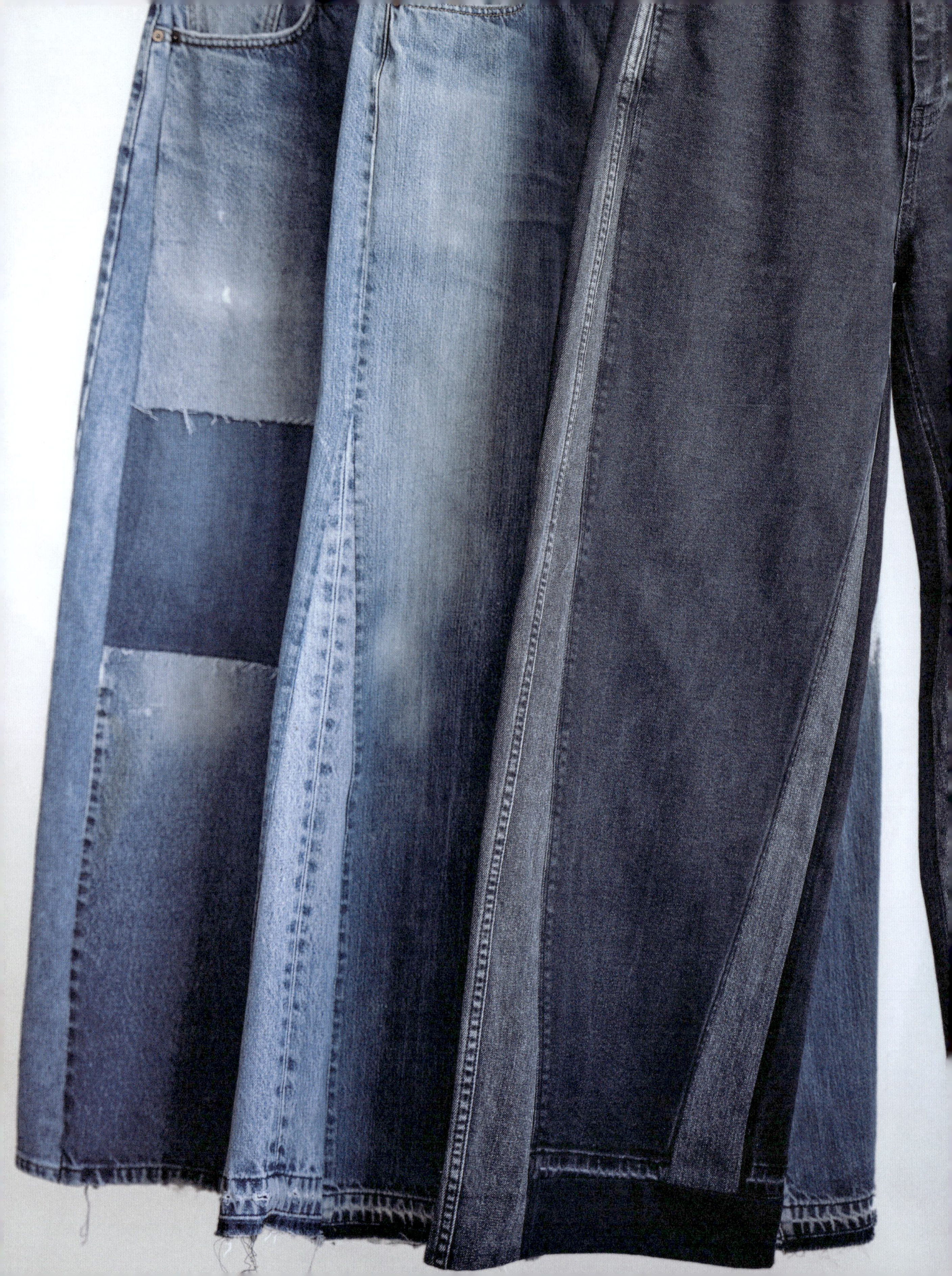

ADDING LEG INSERTS

YOU WILL NEED

- A pair of straight, slim or tapered jeans that fit you on the waist
- A second pair of 'donor' jeans for the inserts

- Tape measure and ruler
- Tailor's chalk or fabric marker
- Fabric shears
- Thread snips
- Seam ripper
- Scalpel
- Pins or sewing clips
- All-purpose threads
- Heavy-duty topstitch threads
- Sewing machine
- Zipper foot
- Denim sewing-machine needles
- Steam iron

There are so many creative ways to reshape your jeans by adding inserts to the leg. In this section, we'll show you how to widen or flare your jeans by sewing in wedge inserts either all the way to the waistband or in shorter sections from the knee or thigh.

Once you've nailed these techniques, you can dive into experimenting with endless shapes, denim combinations and unique details to create a bespoke statement piece.

HOW TO FOLLOW THIS TUTORIAL

1 Use the planning pages on 86–87 to design your style. The diagrams show how common leg shapes can be remodelled and what length and placement of wedge inserts to use.

2 Follow the step-by-step instructions on pages 88–93 to take you through the technical process.

PLANNING YOUR DESIGN

Starting with a slim, straight or tapered fit, use the style guide opposite to explore design options for your jeans. Once you've decided on the design, make a note of the recommended hem circumference* and the type and length of wedge insert needed, for example thigh wedge, knee wedge or full-length insert, before moving to the next section.

Non-stretch or slight-stretch jeans work best. If you are making the wide or flared style avoid any that have a felled side seam. For donor jeans, choose a similar weight and elasticity to your main pair.

* Hem circumferences shown are based on sizes Small, Medium and Large. Add 2cm (¾in) per size for each additional increment.

WEDGE INSERT LENGTHS

Full-length wedge starting at the waist: equal to the whole side-seam length, excluding the waistband.

Short wedge starting at mid-thigh: equal to the distance from hem to halfway between the knee and crotch.

Short wedge starting at the knee: equal to the distance from hem to the top of the kneecap.

STRAIGHTEN

SHORT WEDGE INSERT STARTING AT MID-THIGH

Hem circumference equal or slightly less than your thigh measurement.

WIDEN

FULL-LENGTH WEDGE STARTING AT THE WAIST

SHORT WEDGE STARTING MID-THIGH

	Hem circumference for classic wide leg: 50–60cm (19¾–23⅝in).
	Hem circumference for wide and baggy: 60–66cm (23⅝–26in).

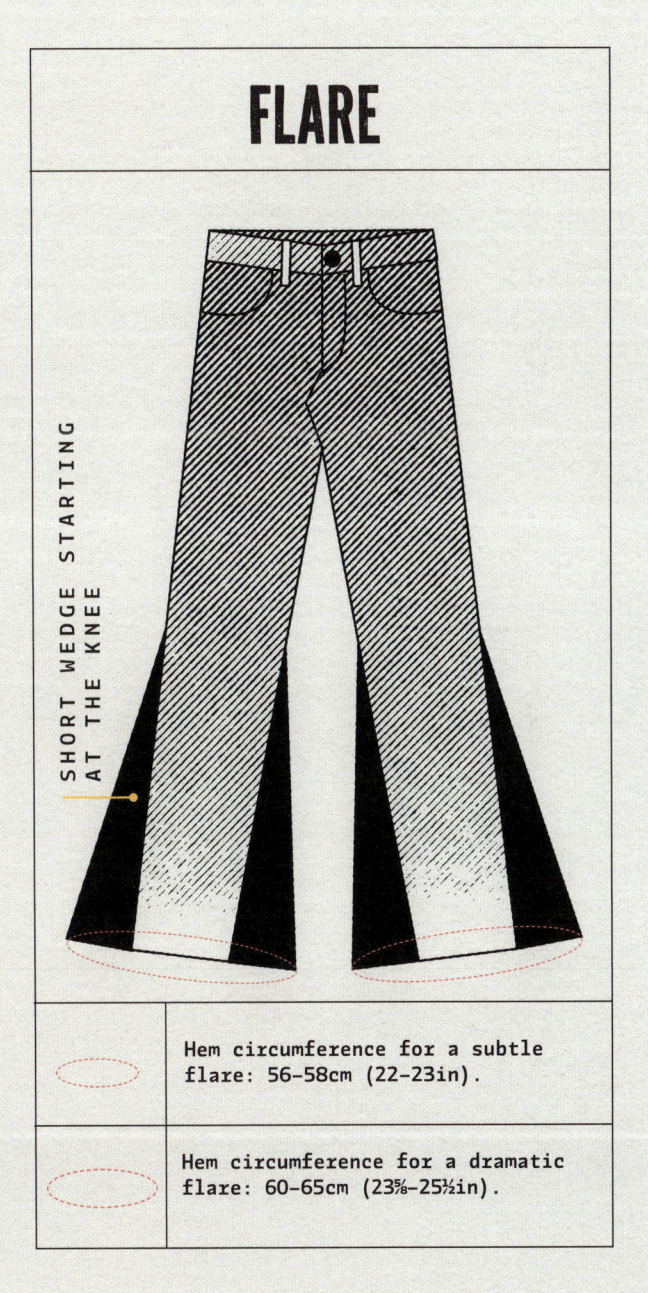

FLARE

SHORT WEDGE STARTING AT THE KNEE

	Hem circumference for a subtle flare: 56–58cm (22–23in).
	Hem circumference for a dramatic flare: 60–65cm (23⅝–25½in).

87

PREPARING THE WEDGE INSERTS

Use the planning guide on pages 86–87 to calculate the difference between the original and new hem circumference. If your jeans have two inserts, divide the number evenly between the two panels.

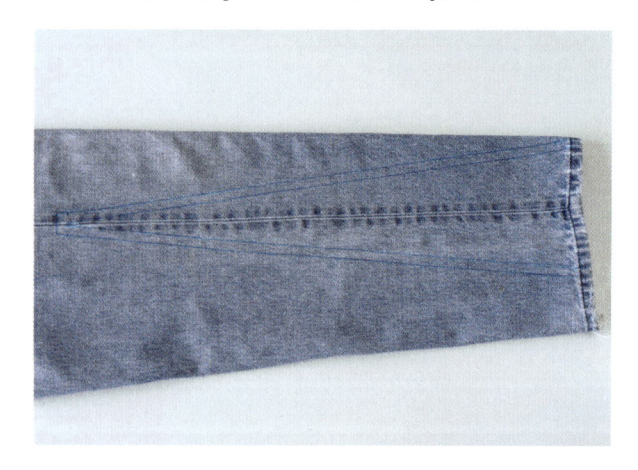

1 Take the donor pair of jeans and, with tailor's chalk or a fabric marker, mark the insert width on the hem, plot the length, joining the sides into a wedge shape. Add a 1cm (⅜in) seam allowance onto the sides.

2 Mark a notch on the seam allowance at both sides of the point. Now mark a dot to show where the point is on the reverse side of the fabric. Cut out the insert.

3 Snip the notches at either side of the point.

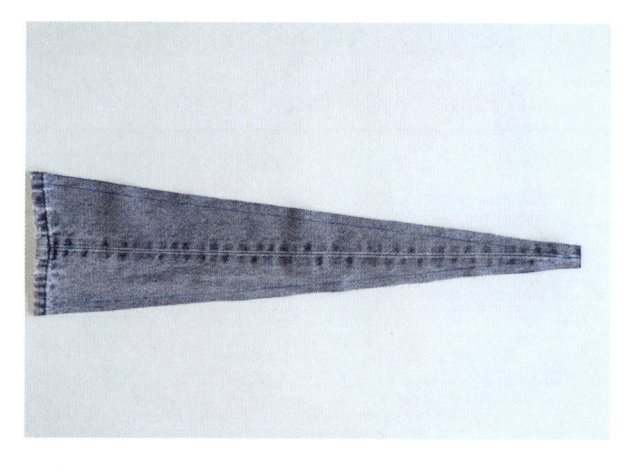

4 Repeat the process for the number of wedge inserts needed for your alteration.

OPENING THE SEAMS

Make a note of the type of seams and stitching on your jeans inside leg and side seams using the jeans anatomy guide on pages 30–31 before starting.

1 Open the hem of both the main pair of jeans and the wedge inserts and then press.

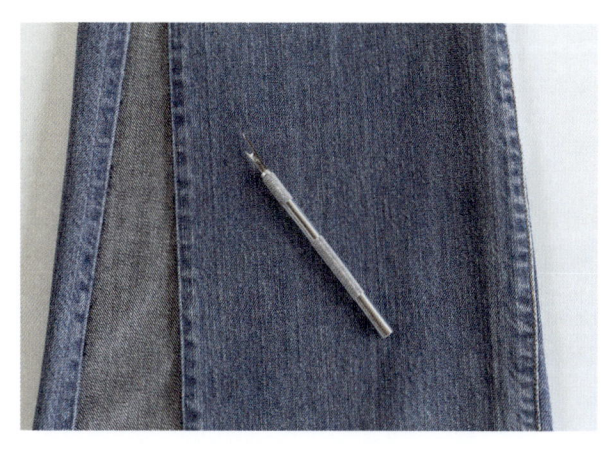

2 For short wedge inserts starting at mid-thigh or the knee, open the seam to around 4cm (1½in) above where the insert ends. Refer to page 33 for how to open the stitching on your seams.

3 To insert a full-length wedge in the side seam, open it all the way to the top and unpick the bottom edge of the waistband 4cm (1½in) either side of the side seam.

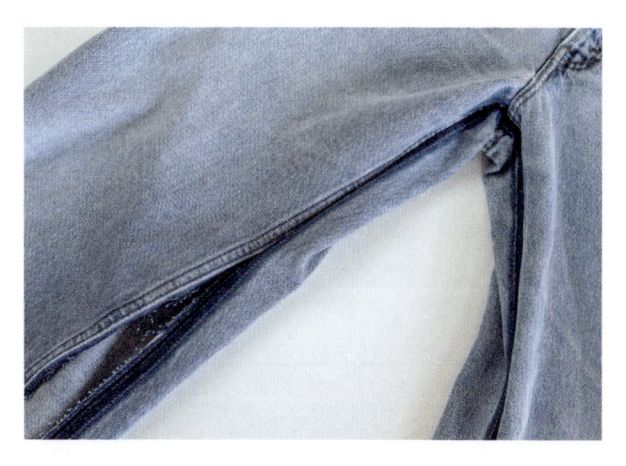

4 To add inserts to a fully felled inside leg seam, include this extra step. Open the inside leg seam all the way around, from hem to hem. Trim 5mm (³⁄₁₆in) off the seam allowance. With the jeans inside out, pin the crotch back together and re-stitch the seam with 1cm (⅜in) seam allowance, starting 4cm (1½in) above where your wedge panel will end and running to the same point on the opposite leg.

INSERTING THE WEDGES

If you are adding more than one wedge insert, do the one on the inside leg first. The following sections explain how to insert your wedge, whether it's short or full-length.

1 Mark the notches on both sides of the seam to match the notches on the wedge. Starting with the front seam and with the jeans right side out, align the notches at the top, pin or clip the front sides together with right sides facing and stitch from the notch down to the hem with a 1cm (3/8in) seam allowance. Press the seams firmly to the front.

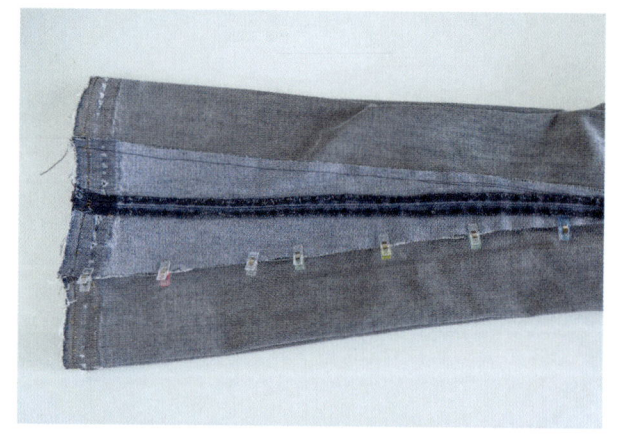

2 Next, turn the jeans inside out to sew the back seams. Pin or clip your wedge to the side seam with right sides facing.

3 Sew from the notch to the hem with the wedge on top. I find sewing on the wedge side so you can see the point markings at the top really helps.

4 Overlock or zigzag stitch along the raw edges of the seams and press them to the outside before turning the jeans inside out and pressing again.

5 If you have more wedges to insert on the same leg, do so according to the instructions for that type of wedge and, if not, you can repeat the steps for the second leg. Finally, press and restitch your hems using topstitch thread and a heavy-duty needle. Or you can leave the hems undone if you prefer.

SEWING IN A FULL-LENGTH WEDGE
This style of insert goes all the way up to the waistband, making the sewing part a little easier as there is no awkward point to incorporate.

Follow steps 1–5 of the instructions for inserting a wedge. Finally, place your side seam back into the waistband and redo the stitching with topstitch thread and a heavy-duty needle.

PLAY AROUND WITH CREATIVE DETAILS

Experiment with mixing sewn-up hems with undone hems/raw edges.

Unpick seams or pockets to reveal indigo shadow details.

While your jeans are open, why not add some knee patches?

Try adding panels with seam details from the original jean – for example, yoke or side seams.

93

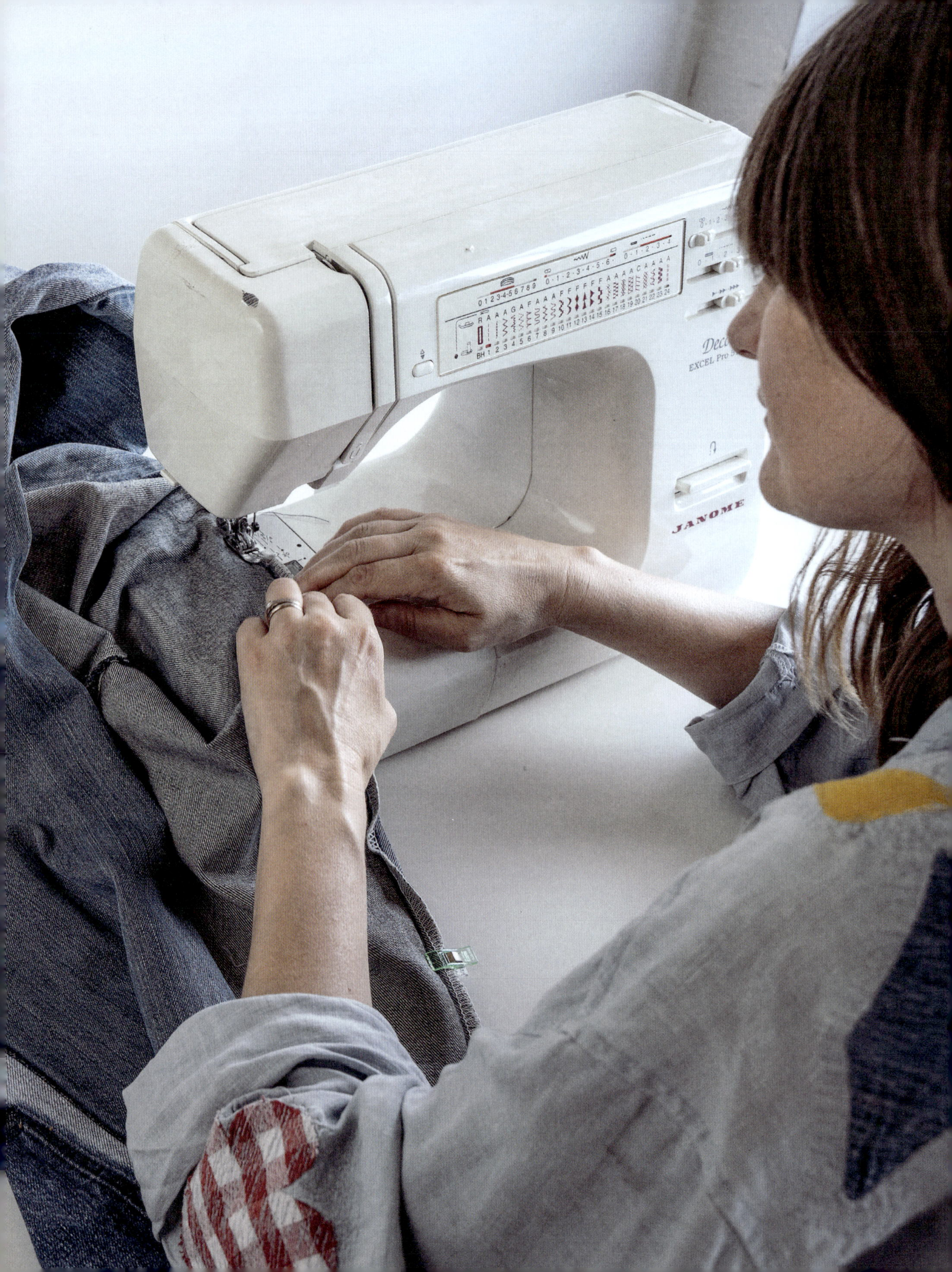
JANOME

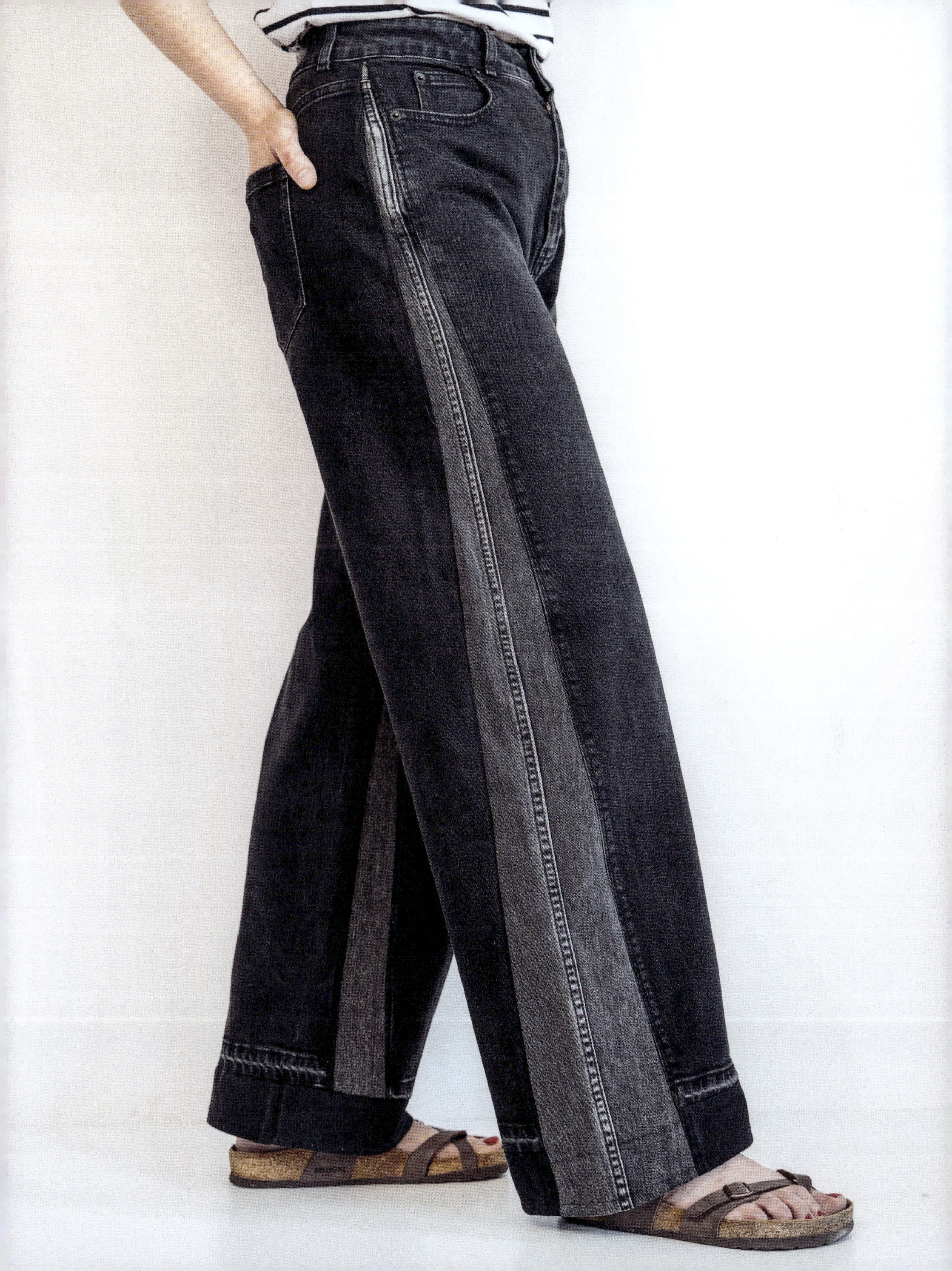

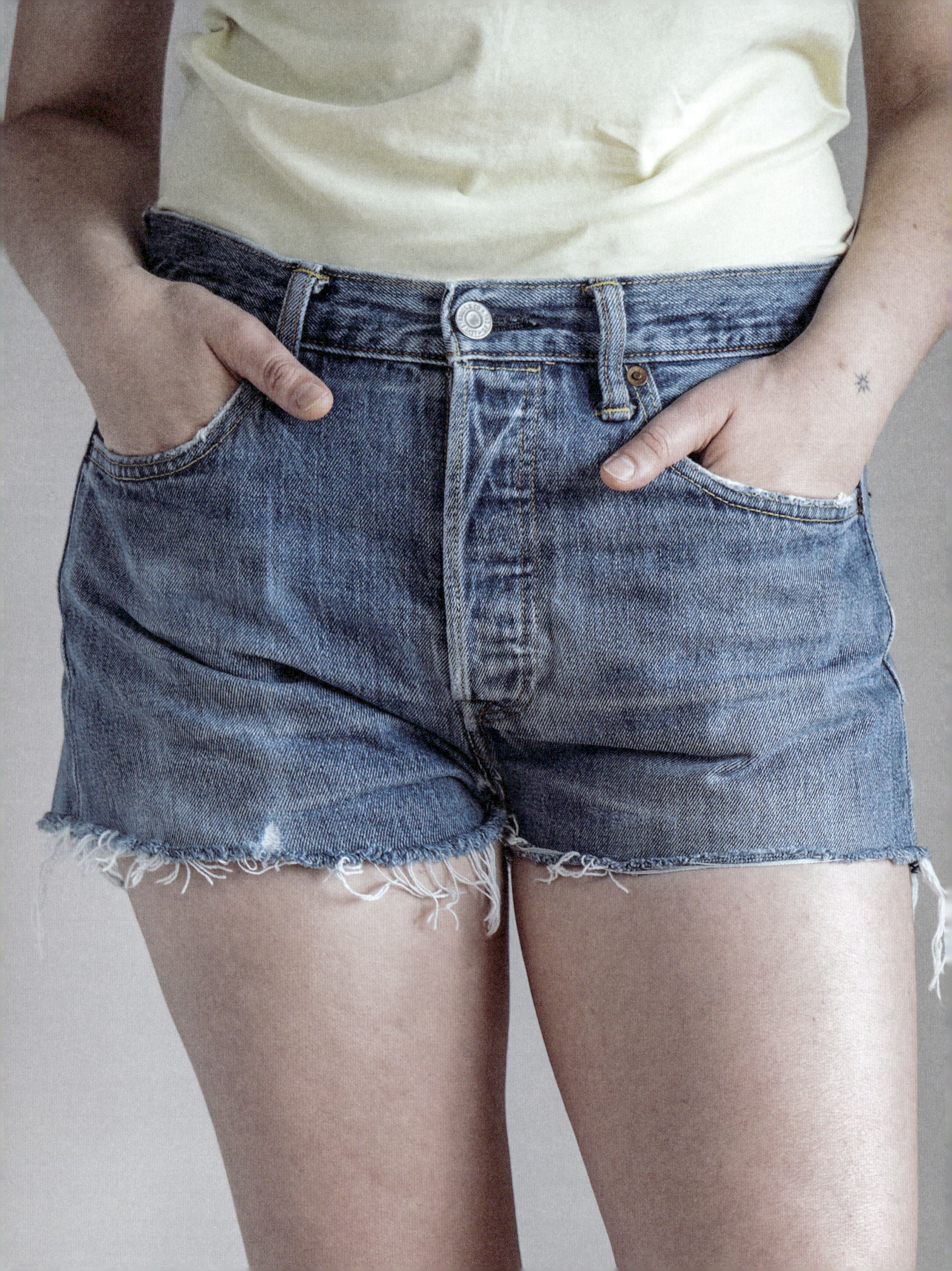

SKILL LEVEL	Basic
MAKE TIME	15 Mins

JEANS TO SHORTS

YOU WILL NEED

- A pair of jeans
- Tape measure and ruler
- Tailor's chalk or fabric marker
- Fabric shears
- Seam ripper

Denim cut-offs, or 'jorts' as they've become known, are one of the quickest and easiest ways to upcycle your jeans; just two quick snips and you're off... well, almost. It's not quite that simple! If you've attempted shorts in the past and weren't thrilled with the results or you're nervous about messing up, don't worry – you're not alone.

In the next few pages you'll discover important tips that will give you the confidence to make the chop. You'll be guided through three different shorts styles: iconic denim hot pants, classic cut-offs and knee-length jorts, explaining all you need to know about shape and measurements along the way. It's a no-sew project so you'll only need a few basic items to get started. In less than the time it takes to cook a pizza, your jeans will be ready for the beach!

CUTTING GUIDE FOR ALL SHORTS STYLES

Hot pants: cut 4cm (1½in) from crotch

Midi cut offs: 19cm (7½in) from crotch

Knee-length jorts: on the knee

HOT PANTS

Start with slim or straight jeans; skinny can also work, but only for the shortest cuts.

1. Measure the desired inside-leg length of the shorts onto the jeans and mark the position on the seam with tailor's chalk. It should be 4cm (1½in) from the crotch for the cheekiest 'Daisy Dukes' and up to 6cm (2⅜in) if you want a bit more coverage.

2. With a tape measure, follow a line from the mark on the inside leg seam across to the side seam, at a right angle to the grain line. Mark this position on the side seam. This style of shorts typically has a slanted cut. To create the slant, measure 4cm (1½in) above the chalk mark on the side seam and draw a new diagonal line across to the inside leg seam mark. Repeat for the other leg.

3. Cut along both lines. If you're unsure, start a bit longer, try them on and turn the edge up to find your ideal length. It's easier to gradually skim a bit more off each time than it is to add it back on, but remember to keep the cut slanted.

CLASSIC CUT-OFFS

For these casual wardrobe staples, start with a pair of straight or wide-leg jeans.

1. Measure 19cm (7½in) from the crotch down the inside leg seam and mark with chalk.

2. Draw a line from this mark across to the side seam at a right angle to the grain line. Cut along the line. Repeat steps 1 and 2 for the other leg.

3. If you want them to be cuffed, turn the shorts up 3.5cm (1⅜in), twice. If you like, you can press the turn-up but if you prefer a more casual cuff then leave it unpressed.

THE DISTRESSED LOOK

From a gently frayed hem to full-on rips, creative patches and repairs – there's so much you can do to add detail to your shorts. Dive into the Repair section (pages 47–75) for inspiration and learn how to create an authentic frayed look on page 43.

KNEE-LENGTH JORTS

Jorts are the ultimate come-back kid of denim. Long and loose, they pivot easily between laid-back style and nostalgic cool. Turning your old jeans into jorts isn't just an upcycling flex – it's a way to rock a look that screams 'too cool to care'.

1. Put the jeans on and find the position of the top of your kneecap. Mark this at the inseam with chalk
2. Take the jeans off and lie them flat, front-side up. Draw a line from the mark on the inside leg seam across to the side seam at a right angle to the grain line. This will be your finished length.
3. Cut along this line or a little longer, if you want to test it out first. Repeat steps 1–3 for the other leg.
4. Try the shorts on and mark any adjustments. Trim if needed before fraying the edges (see page 43).

> If your starting jeans are too slim or if you'd like a baggier fit, you could add a full-length wedge insert in the side seam (shown in the photo above) by following the instructions on pages 84–93. For this look, aim for a hem circumference of 60–65cm (23⅜–25½in).

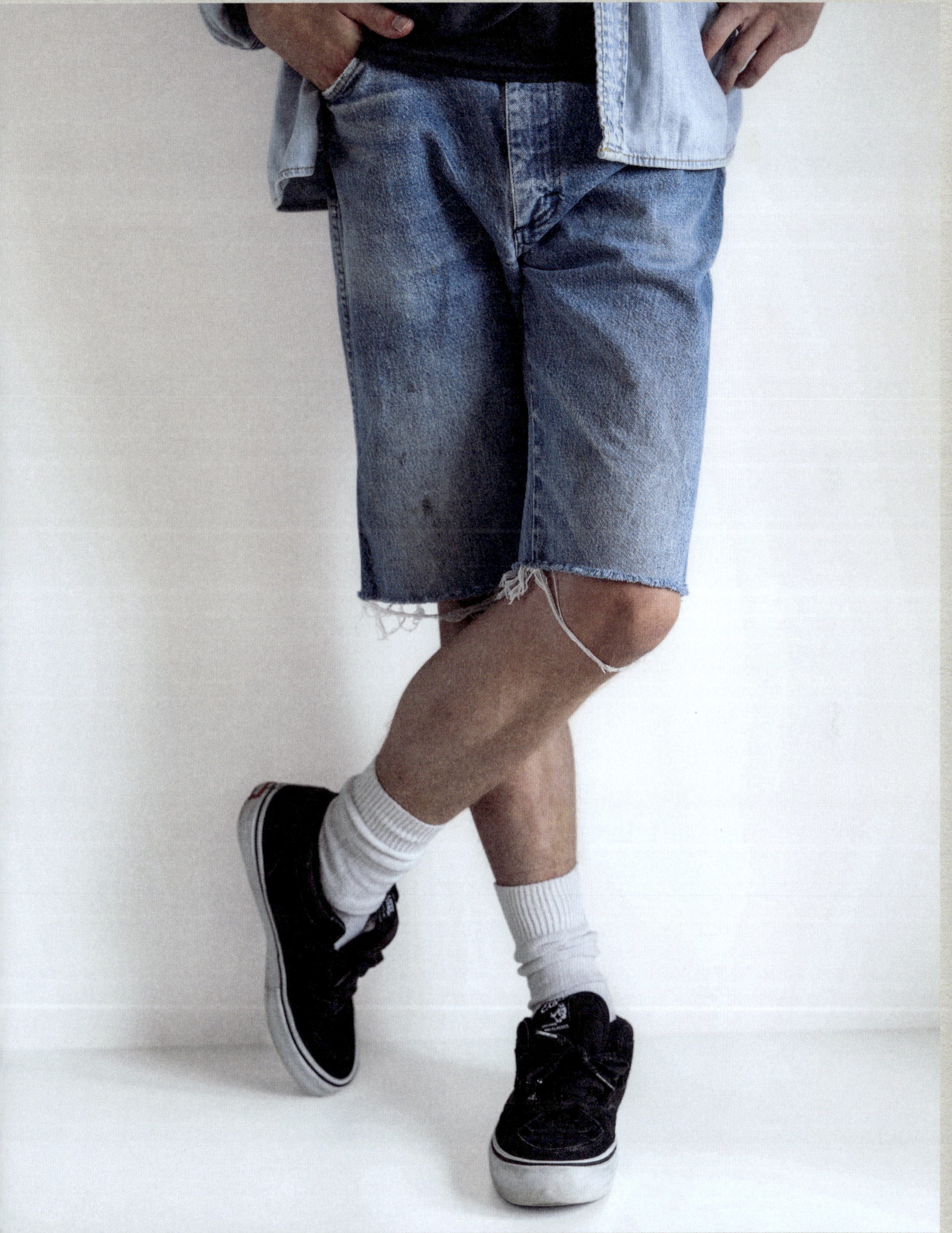

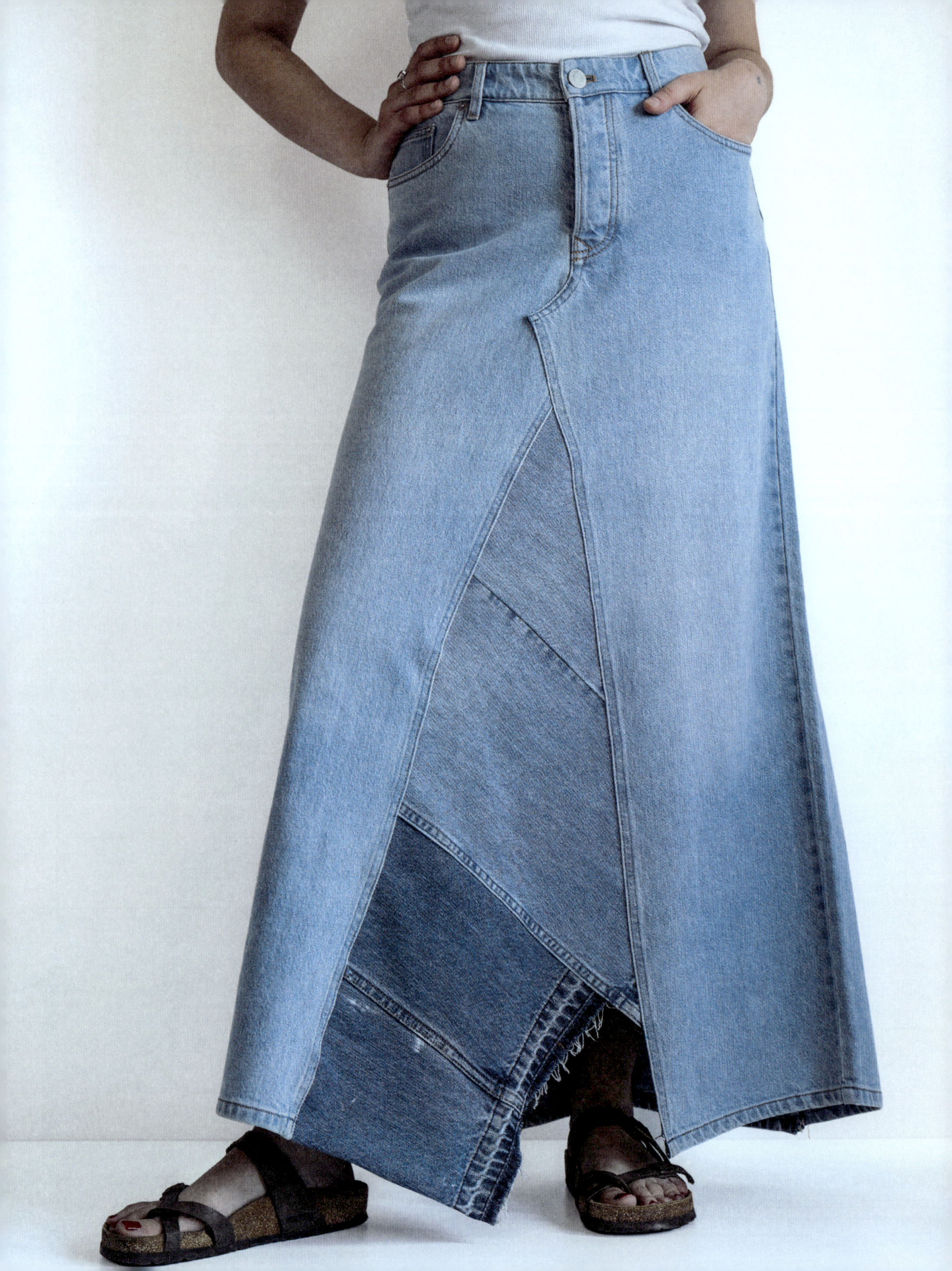

SKILL LEVEL	Medium
MAKE TIME	1.5 Hours

JEANS TO SKIRT

YOU WILL NEED

- 1 pair of old jeans (works best on non-stretch or low stretch)
- 2 x cut-off jeans legs (similar weight and elasticity to the main pair)
- Thread snips
- Seam ripper
- Pins or sewing clips
- Tailor's chalk or fabric marker
- Ruler
- Fabric shears
- All-purpose threads
- Heavy-duty topstitch threads
- Sewing machine
- Denim sewing-machine needles
- Steam iron

With this fun technique, you can turn your old jeans into a denim skirt – mini or maxi – in just over an hour. It's a quick, creative project that rewards you with something way cooler than anything off the rack. Denim skirts are the perfect mix of vintage style and DIY charm, plus, with millions of jeans ending up in landfill every year, upcycling is a smart and conscious way to tackle waste while refreshing your wardrobe.

MAXI SKIRT

1 Open the inside leg seam of your jeans all the way around from one ankle to the other using the guide on page 35. Press the seam allowance on the legs firmly to the inside.

2 Open the front seam from the crotch until the point where the seam curves just below the fly. Open the back rise all the way up to the yoke seam.

3 Lay the garment on a table front side up. Overlap the front pieces at the crotch until the panels lie flat. Pin them in place and topstitch along the original seam lines. Now do the same on the back.

4 To create the inserts, open the cut-off jeans legs on the inside leg seam (you can cut along the seams rather than unpick them). Press them flat.

5 With the garment laid flat on a table front-side up, the legs falling at their natural position, place the panel inside and position it to cover the gap between the legs. Pin the panel in place before stitching along the lines of the original seams. Trim the inserted panel to match the line of the skirt hem if needed.

6 Turn the skirt inside out and trim all seam allowances down to 1.5cm (½in). If you like, you can then finish the edges of the panels with zigzag stitch or overlocking. The stitching should be on the seam allowances only; it should not show through onto the garment. Try your skirt on – check that its comfortable to walk and sit in.

If you started with a slim jean, you may need to add a split in one or both sides. You can do this by opening the side seam up to a point about 15cm (6in) above the knee. Press the seams to the inside and topstitch.

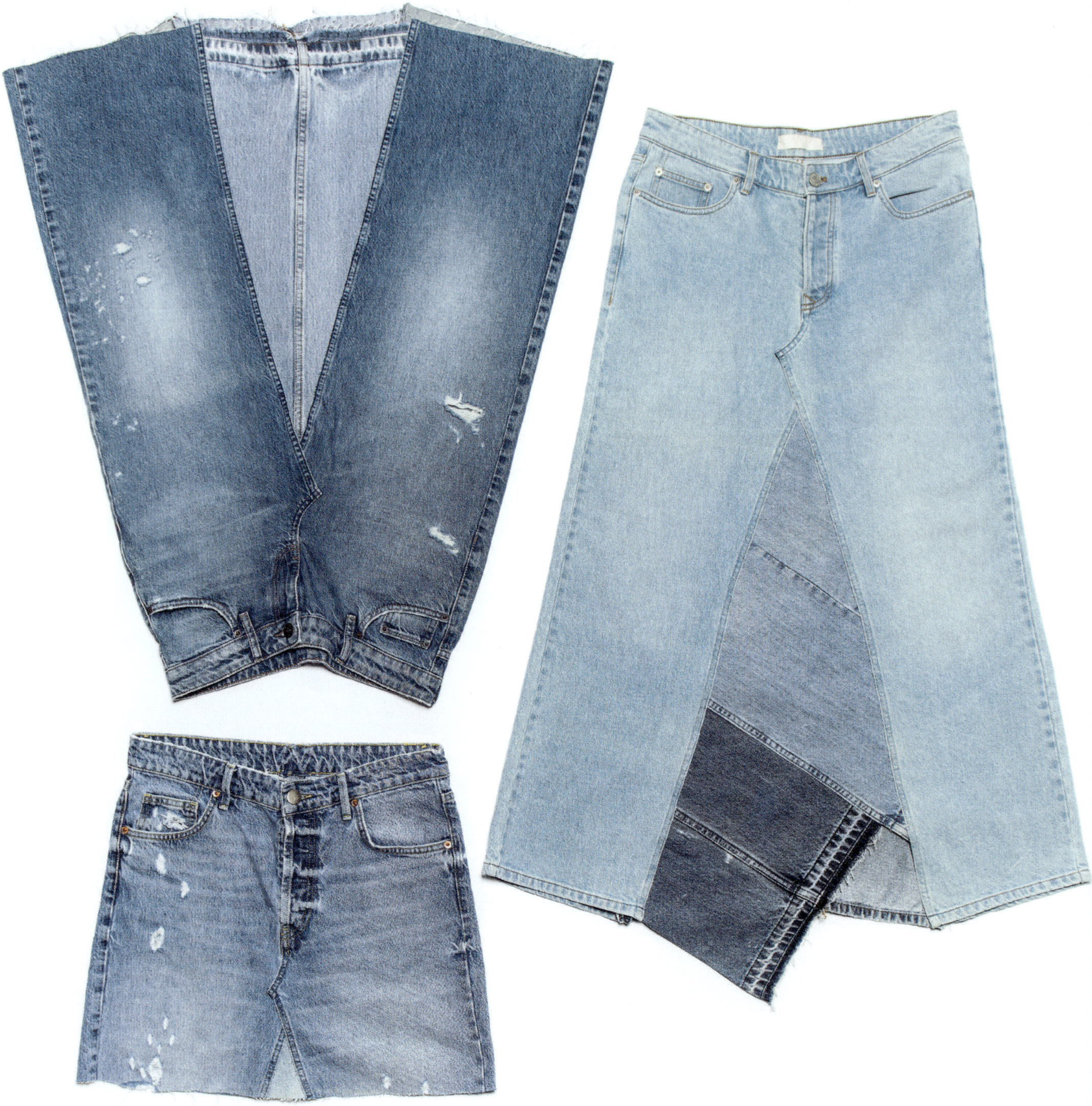

MAKE YOUR GARMENT UNIQUE

Try a split version.

Create a patchwork panel for your inserts and experiment with asymmetric hems.

Unpick and drop the hems on the skirt or the inserted panel.

Leave the seam raw, showing indigo shadows.

MINI SKIRT

This process is almost the same as for the maxi skirt, but you'll need to cut it before starting and again after inserting the panel, if one is needed.

1 Start by measuring 18cm (7in) from the crotch down the inside leg seam and cut the legs off at right angles to the grain line. This is longer than you will need, but it will be shortened later.

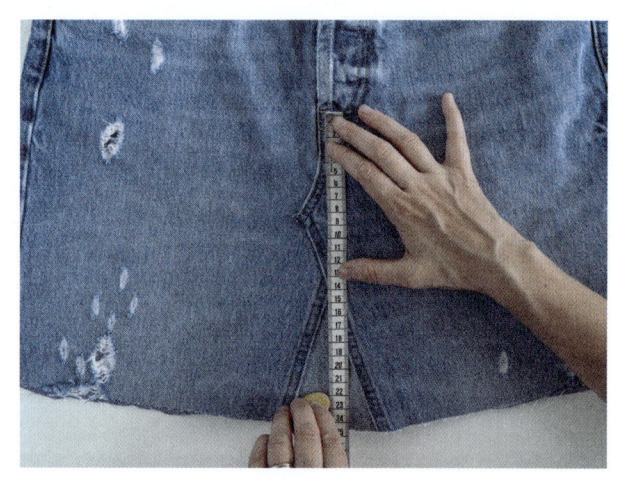

2 Follow steps 2 and 3 on page 104. When you get to step 3, try the pinned skirt on before stitching to check if it needs an insert and also to check the back panels. If the back is jutting out at the hem, overlap the panels a little more. When you're happy with how it looks, secure in place with topstitching.

3 If there is a gap to fill on the hem, take a scrap of denim (it will likely be a very small gap) and follow step 5 on page 105.

4 Lay the skirt front-side up, smoothing it out so the back is not bunched up. Measure 22cm (8½in) down from the bar tack on the fly and mark it with chalk. Follow this line out to the side seams at a right angle to the centre front fly. Mark with chalk and trim the front and back hems together.

Fray the hem gently (see page 43) or let it unravel naturally as the skirt ages.

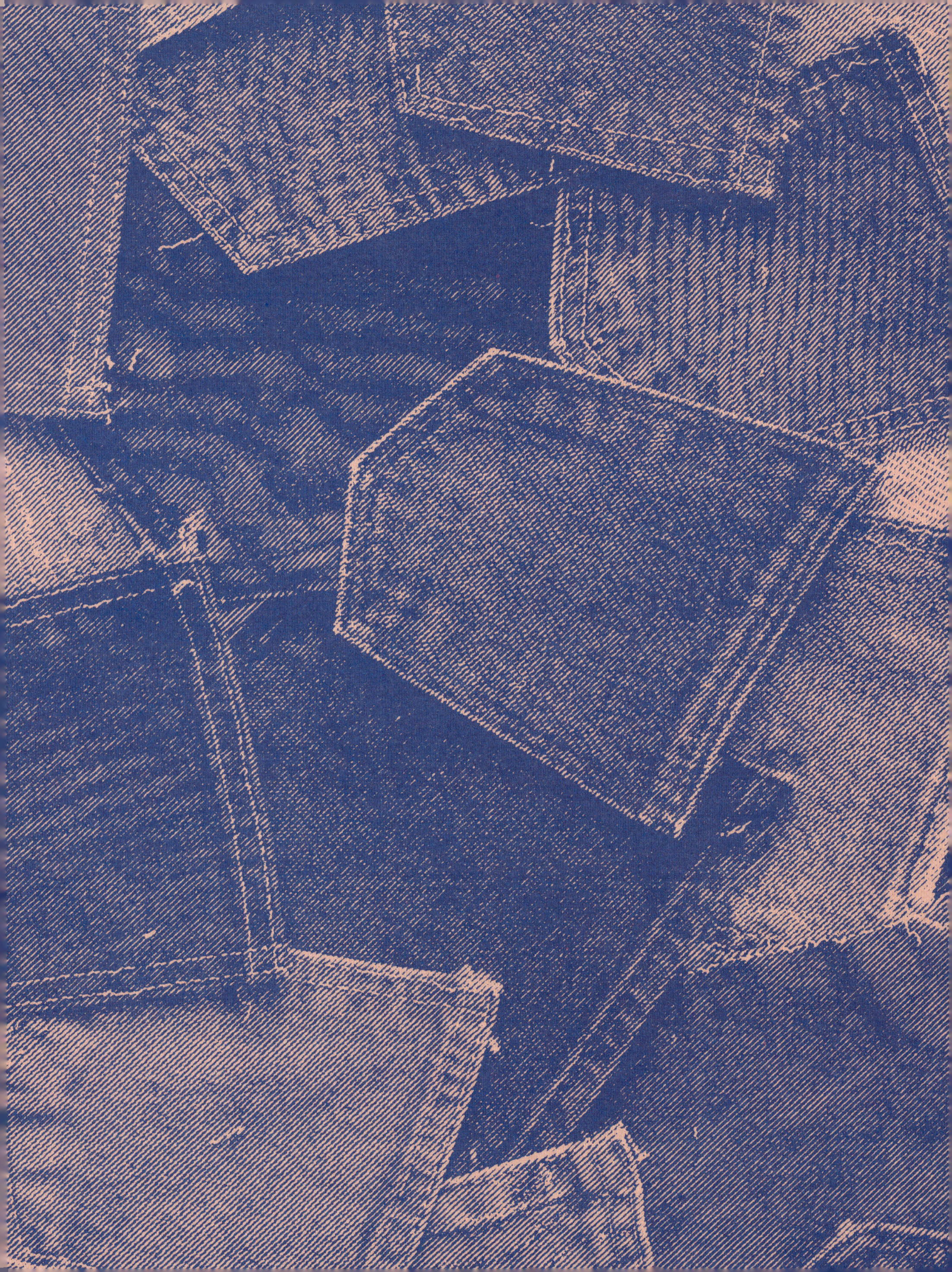

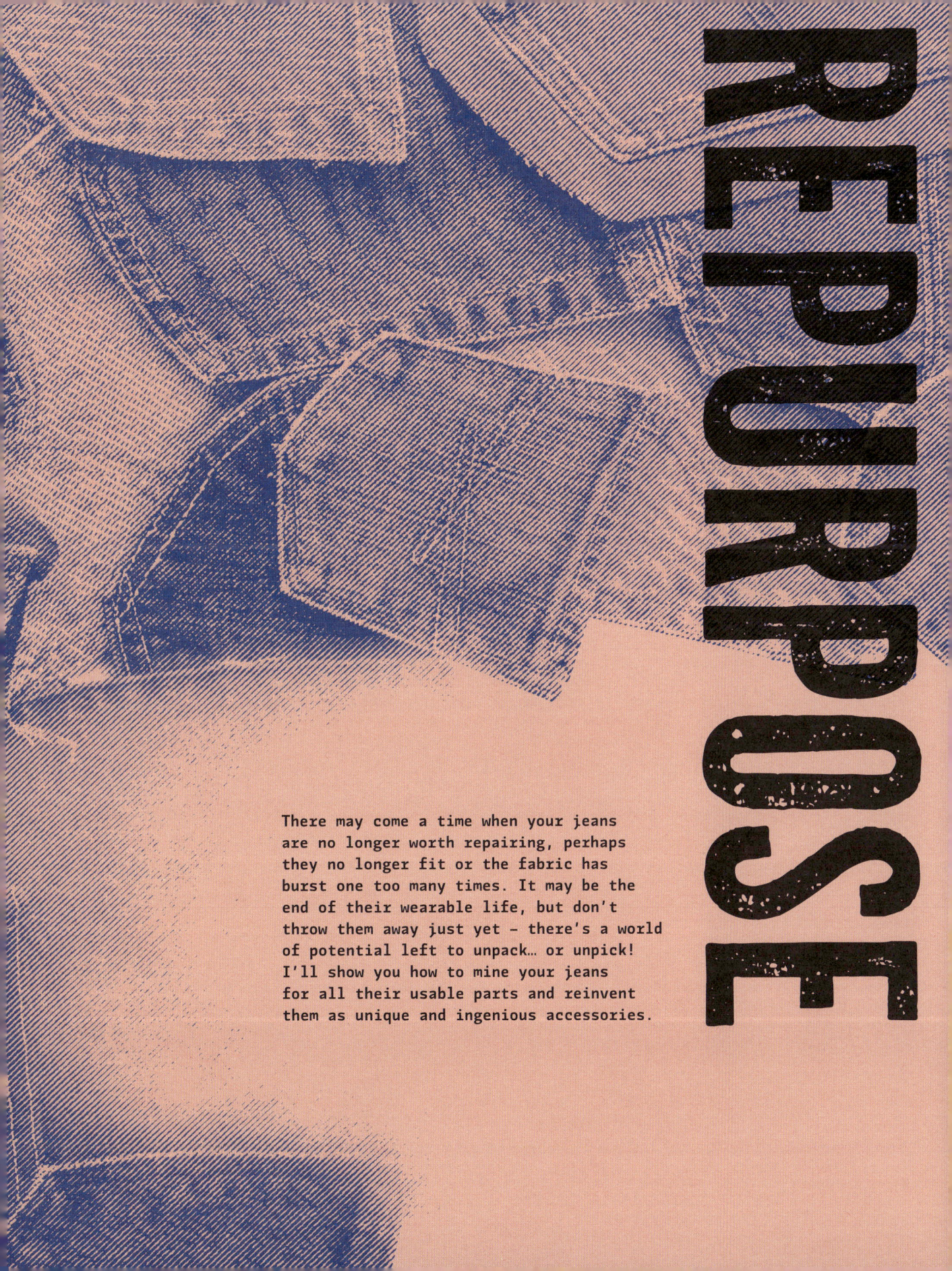

REPURPOSE

There may come a time when your jeans are no longer worth repairing, perhaps they no longer fit or the fabric has burst one too many times. It may be the end of their wearable life, but don't throw them away just yet – there's a world of potential left to unpack… or unpick! I'll show you how to mine your jeans for all their usable parts and reinvent them as unique and ingenious accessories.

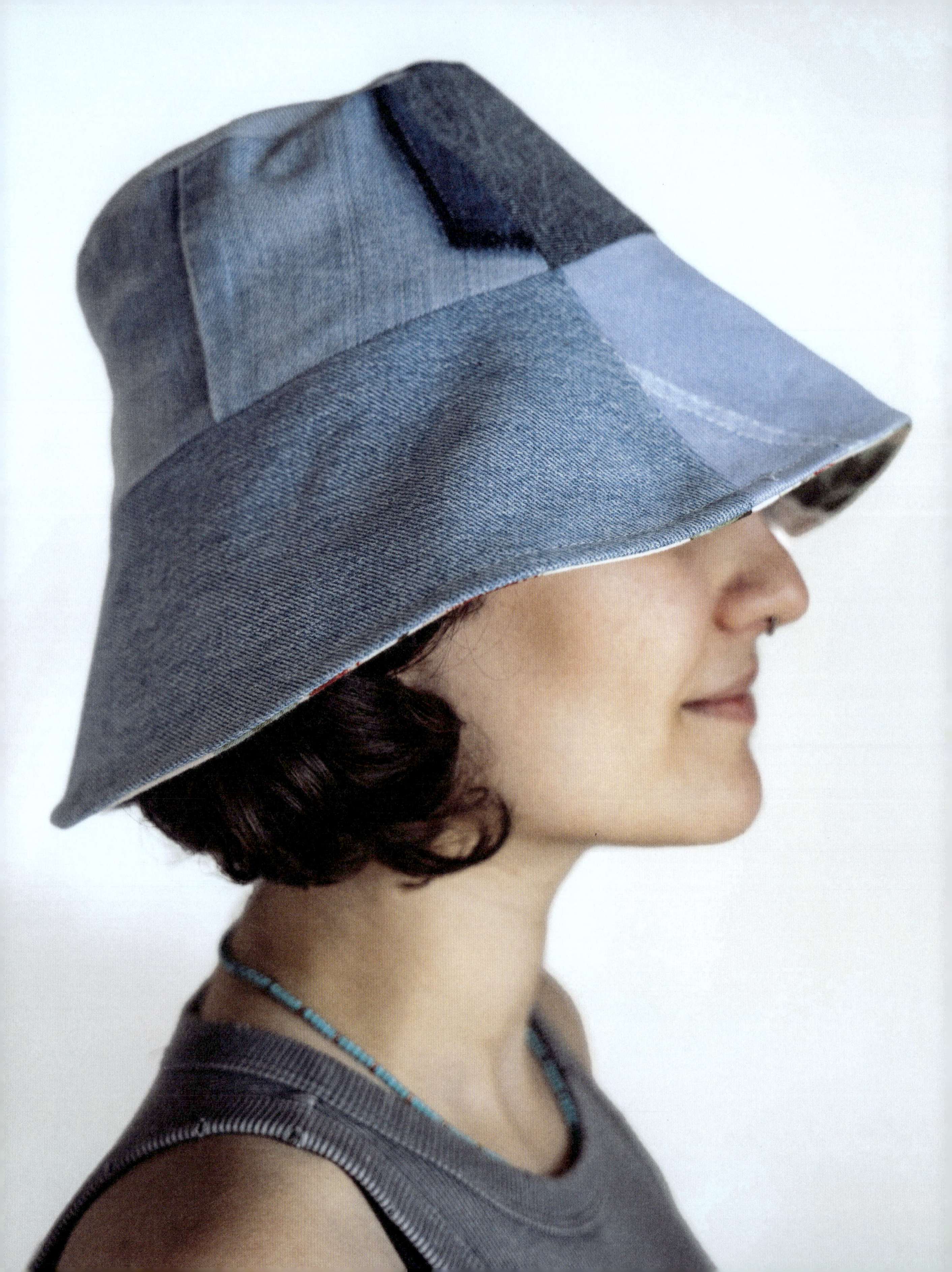

SKILL LEVEL	Medium
MAKE TIME	2 Hours
FINISHED SIZE	Head circumference 54-58cm (21-23in)

REVERSIBLE SUNHAT

YOU WILL NEED

- One leg from a pair of non-stretch jeans or equivalent in denim scraps
- 30cm (12in) of repurposed lining fabric such as old curtains, pillowcases or cushion covers
- Paper, pencil, ruler and scissors for making the pattern
- Pins or sewing clips
- Fabric shears
- Tailor's chalk or fabric marker
- All-purpose threads
- Sewing machine
- Thread snips
- Steam iron

This is a wonderful way to transform small denim scraps into a statement accessory. For me, the most exciting part is deciding which details to incorporate. I like to experiment with seams and shadow details revealed by unpicking the pockets. Due to the strong curves in the pattern, this hat works best with non-stretch fabrics.

PATTERN : REVERSIBLE SUNHAT

BRIM

CUT 2 X DENIM
CUT 2 X LINING

Trace or photocopy the pattern pieces, cut them out and pin them to the folded fabric, with the dotted line placed along the fold.

Cut through both layers of fabric and then open out. Notch the centre on the fold line – there are quarter notches on the crown that match to the side seams.

CUT ON FOLD

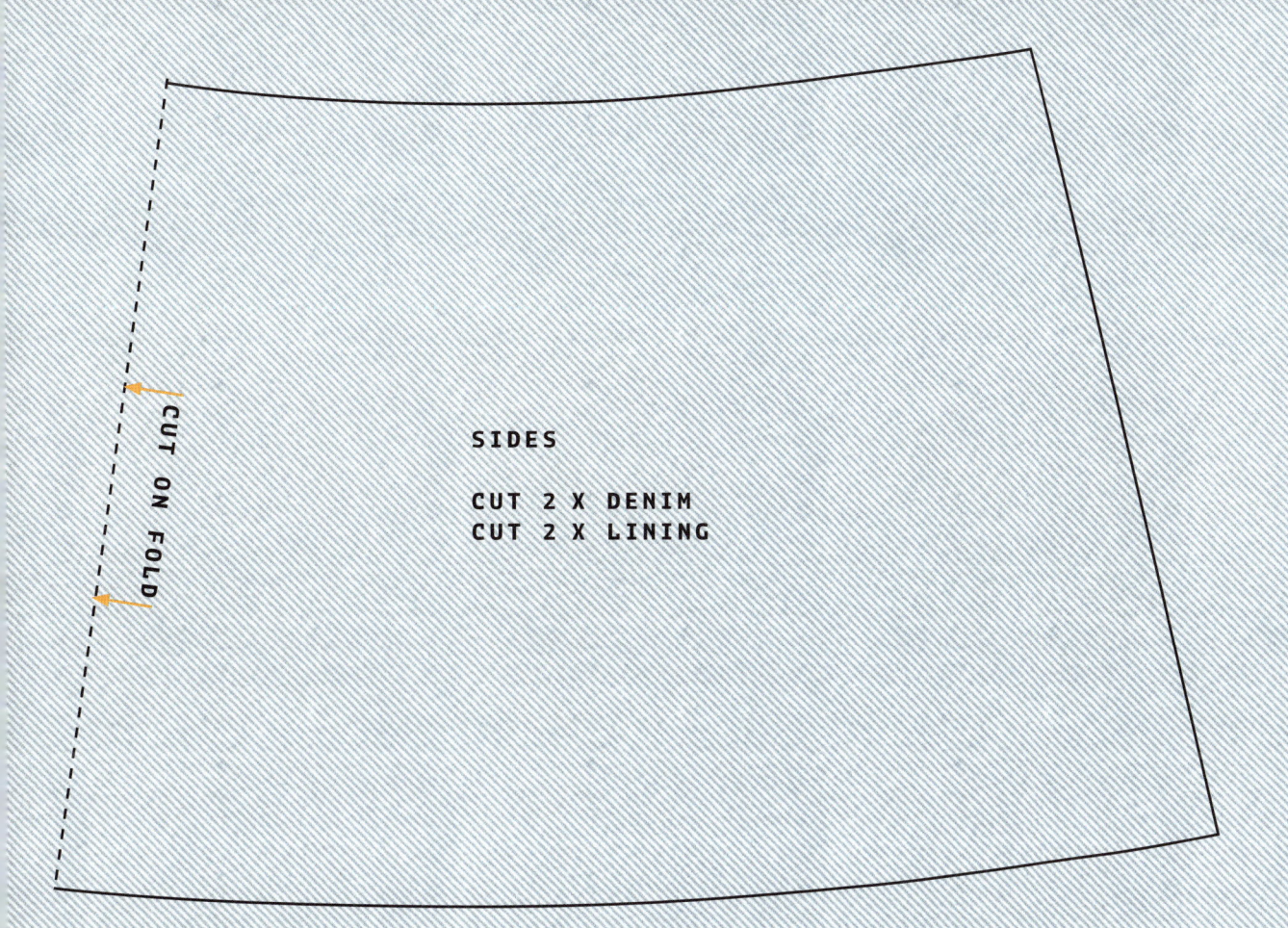

CUT ON FOLD

SIDES

CUT 2 X DENIM
CUT 2 X LINING

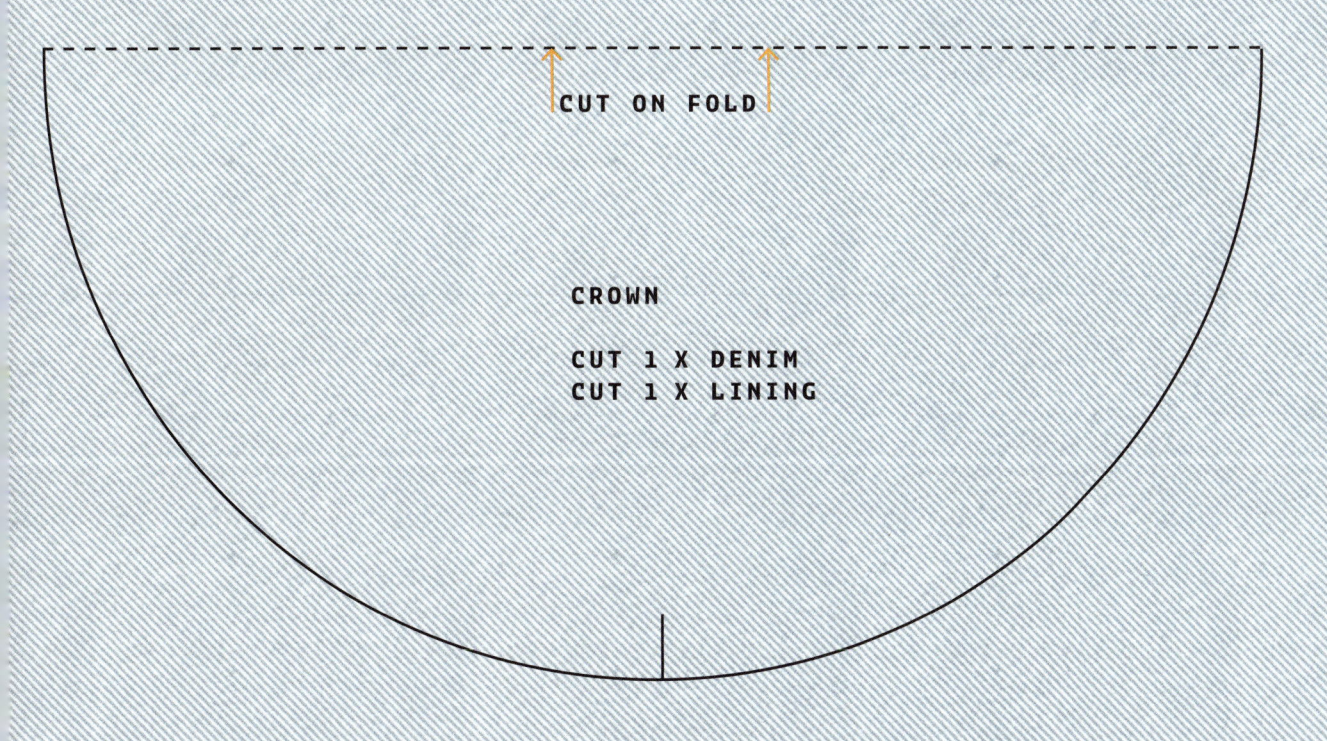

CUT ON FOLD

CROWN

CUT 1 X DENIM
CUT 1 X LINING

REVERSIBLE SUNHAT

1 Cut the pieces from your fabric using the pattern and instructions on pages 114–115. Cut them from the main fabric and the lining fabric. Mark notches.

2 Place the side panels together with right sides facing and stitch up the side seams with 1cm (⅜in) seam allowance. Press the seams open.

3 Now take the brim and brim lining and stitch the side seams together in the same way that you did for the sides. Press the seams open.

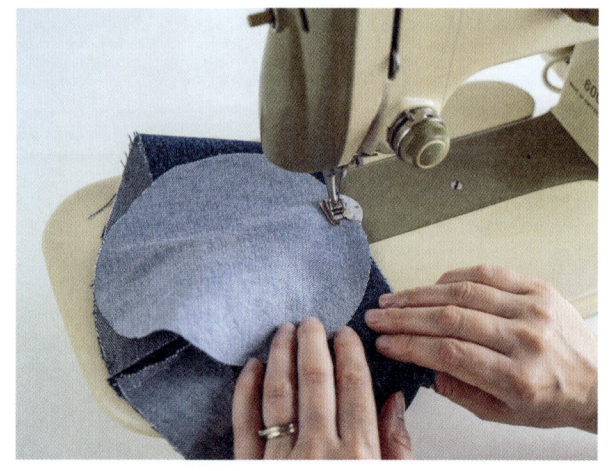

4 Place the stitched side piece and the crown with right sides together. With the side piece on the bottom and crown piece on top, stitch slowly around the circumference, joining the pieces. This is the trickiest step; take it slowly, use all the notches and compensate immediately if one doesn't match up. I find this easier without pins, but if you are not comfortable without them, use them one at a time just for the notch in front of you. Press the seams onto the side panel.

5 Place the brim piece onto the sides with right sides facing and sew them together with a 1cm (⅜in) seam allowance. Press the seam allowance upwards towards the brim.

6 Place the brim lining onto the brim with right sides facing and sew them together around the circumference with a 1cm (⅜in) seam allowance.

7 Sew the side pieces of the lining together and then sew them to the crown in the same way that you did for the main fabric in steps 2 and 3.

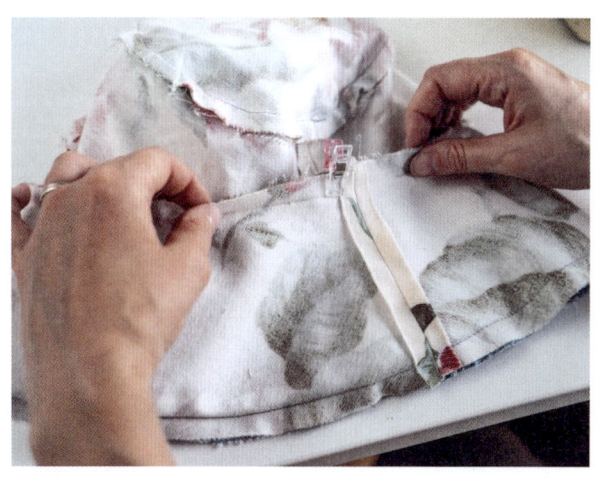

8 Turn the upper part of the lining inside out and place on top of the hat with right sides facing (the main fabric part should be right side up with the brim lining turned to the outside). Sew the upper part of the lining to the brim lining with a 1cm (⅜in) seam allowance, leaving a gap of around 4–5cm (1½–2in) for turning the hat through. Use reverse stitch to secure the ends.

One of my favourite ways to source materials is to post in online groups; I usually find that people are delighted to have an alternative to throwing items in the bin.

117

9 Carefully ease the whole hat through the small gap you left in the previous step.

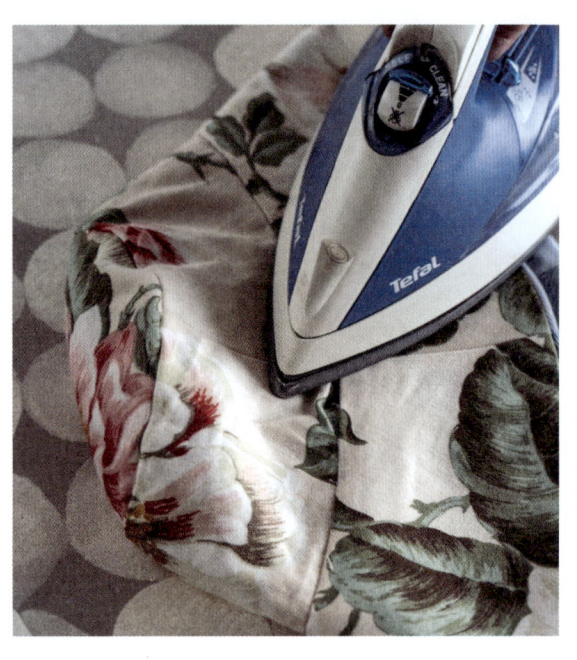

10 Smooth the brim and crown into position and press carefully. Press the seam allowance of the gap neatly inside so you can't see it and hand stitch it to the brim facing with a whip stitch.

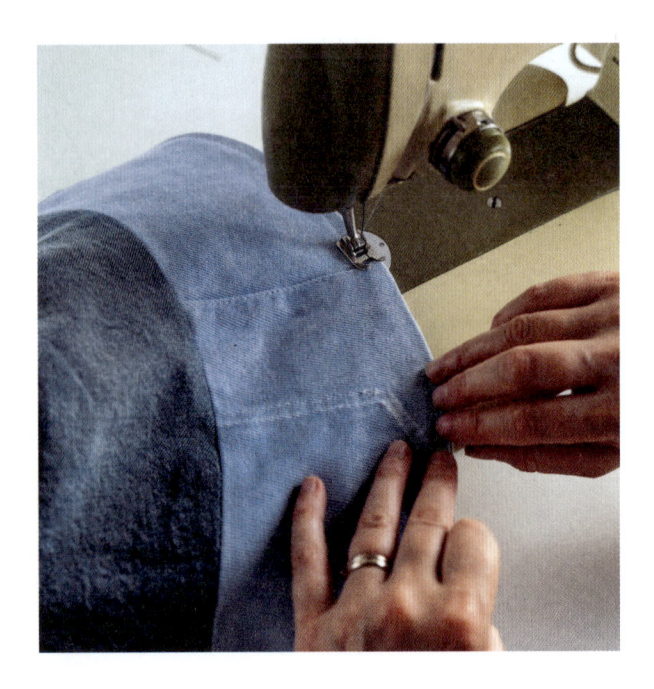

11 Edge stitch the brim about 5mm/³⁄₁₆in (or a sewing-machine's foot width) from the outer edge. Do the same on the seam between the brim and the sides, edge stitching onto the brim.

12 If you wish, you can continue to add stitching in rings, the same width apart, until you have filled the brim. This will help to give the brim more structure, especially helpful if it is floppy.

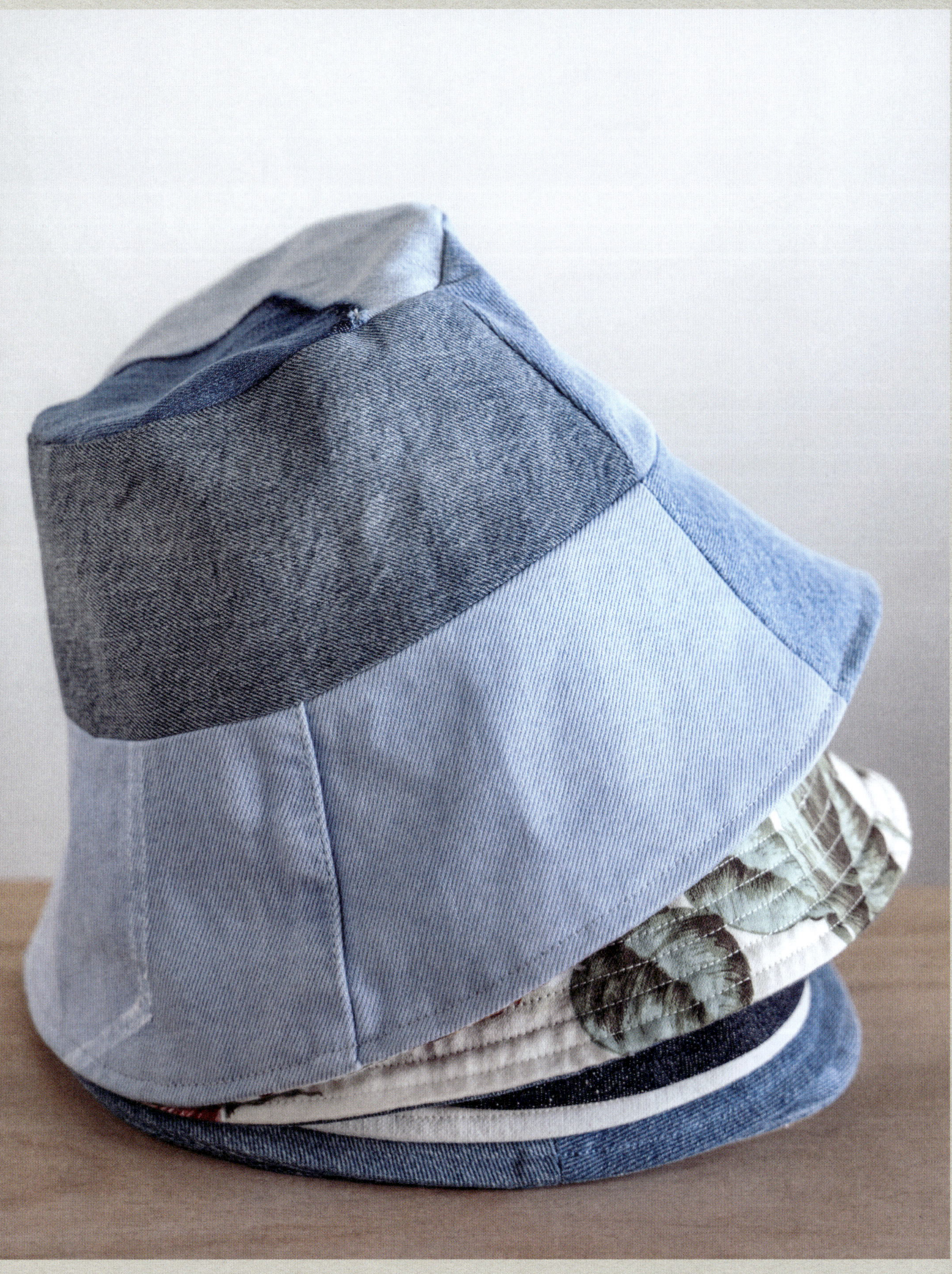

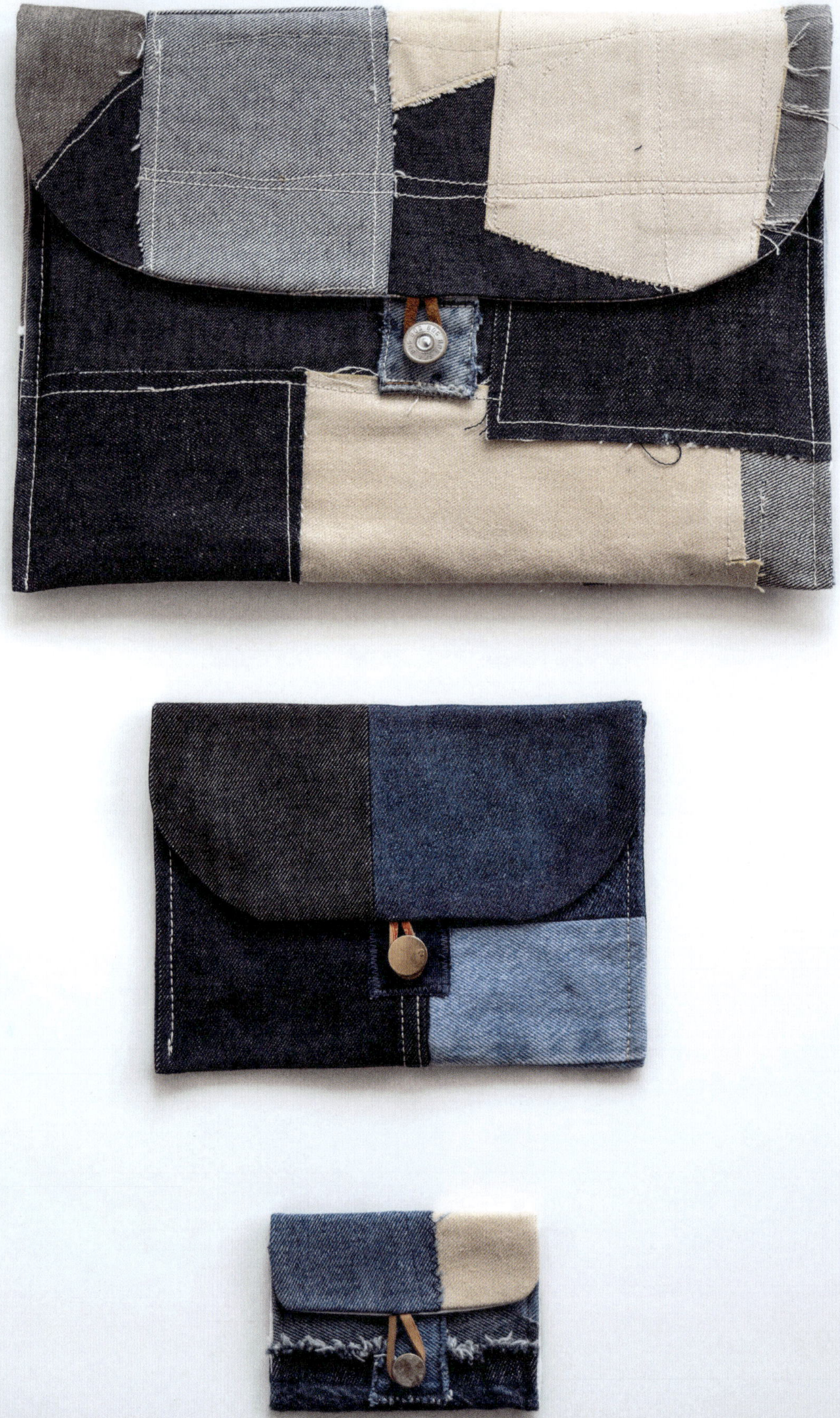

SKILL LEVEL	Basic
MAKE TIME	1.5 Hours (depending on size)
FINISHED SIZE	See size chart on page 122 for options

SCRAP PATCH POUCH

YOU WILL NEED

- Denim scraps – enough to make a piece of fabric bigger than your chosen template size
- Leather or Jacron patch from the back waistband of a pair of jeans (or you can use a 7.5cm/3in length of cord or narrow ribbon)
- Jeans button from waistband, still attached to a square of denim 4 x 4cm (1½ x 1½in) or any sew-on button
- Reclaimed lining fabric from a pillowcase or shirt
- Paper, pencil, ruler and scissors for making the pattern
- Tailor's chalk or fabric marker
- Fabric shears
- Pins or sewing clips
- Sewing machine
- All-purpose threads
- Steam iron
- Zipper foot
- Heavy-duty topstitch threads

This is a versatile project that can be adapted for lots of different uses. With the same technique, you can make a wallet, headphones case, travel pouch or even a laptop case. Some of the smaller pieces take less than an hour so you can turn your scraps into the ideal emergency gift!

PATTERN : SCRAP PATCH POUCH

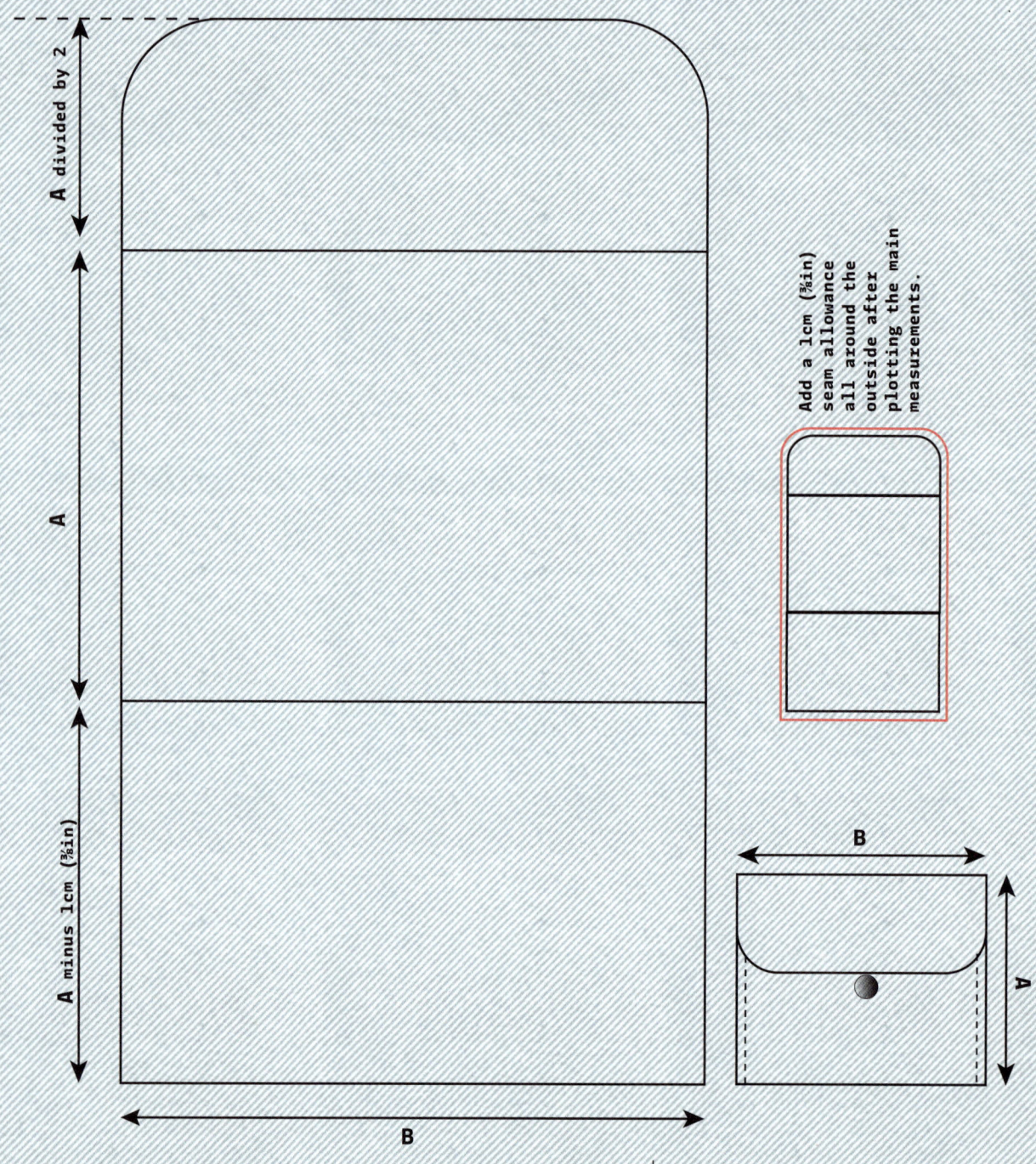

A divided by 2

A

A minus 1cm (⅜in)

Add a 1cm (⅜in) seam allowance all around the outside after plotting the main measurements.

B

B

A

Decide the dimensions of your finished pouch. A is the height and B is the width of your pouch. To work out the length of each section, use the calculations shown above.

ITEM	SIZE
Card wallet	(A)9 × (B)11.5cm (3½ × 4½in)
Cosmetics pouch	(A)16 × (B)21cm (6¼ × 8¼in)
Laptop cover	(A)25 × (B)35cm (9¾ × 13¾in)

1 Make a paper template for your pouch using the information opposite. Choose the size or use your own dimensions. Make a patchwork of denim scraps slightly larger than the pattern using one of the techniques covered on pages 149–153.

2 Use the pattern to mark the shape onto the fabric with chalk and then cut it out. Now do the same for the lining fabric.

3 To make the button loop, trim a strip off the jeans patch, about 7.5cm (3in) long and 3mm (⅛in) wide. If you don't have a jeans patch, use a length of cord or narrow ribbon. Fold it to form a loop and pin it, pointing inwards, to the front side of your patchwork panel at the centre of the flap. Secure it with a row of stitches about 5mm (³⁄₁₆in) from the edge.

4 Place the lining and patchwork with right sides together. Using a sewing machine, stitch all the way around the edge with a 1cm (⅜in) seam allowance, leaving a 5cm (2in) gap on the bottom edge. Snip any pointed corners.

5 Trim the seam allowance down to 5mm (³⁄₁₆in). Turn the pieces inside out through the gap and firmly press all your edges. Use a chopstick or knitting needle to push the corners out. The seam allowance may be bulky in places. Press with an iron, using lots of steam and pressure. Close the gap with a row of topstitching.

6 Fold the finished panel using your pattern to measure the position of the folds. Press it and pin in place. Position the button with waistband scrap still attached on the front. Check that the loop fits around the button and adjust if needed. Pin and sew in place with a zigzag stitch (using a zipper foot if needed).

7 Stitch up both sides of the pouch about 5mm (³⁄₁₆in) from the edge. I like to do this with topstitching thread for extra strength. If your sewing machine is struggling, refer to page 40 for how to manage thick materials.

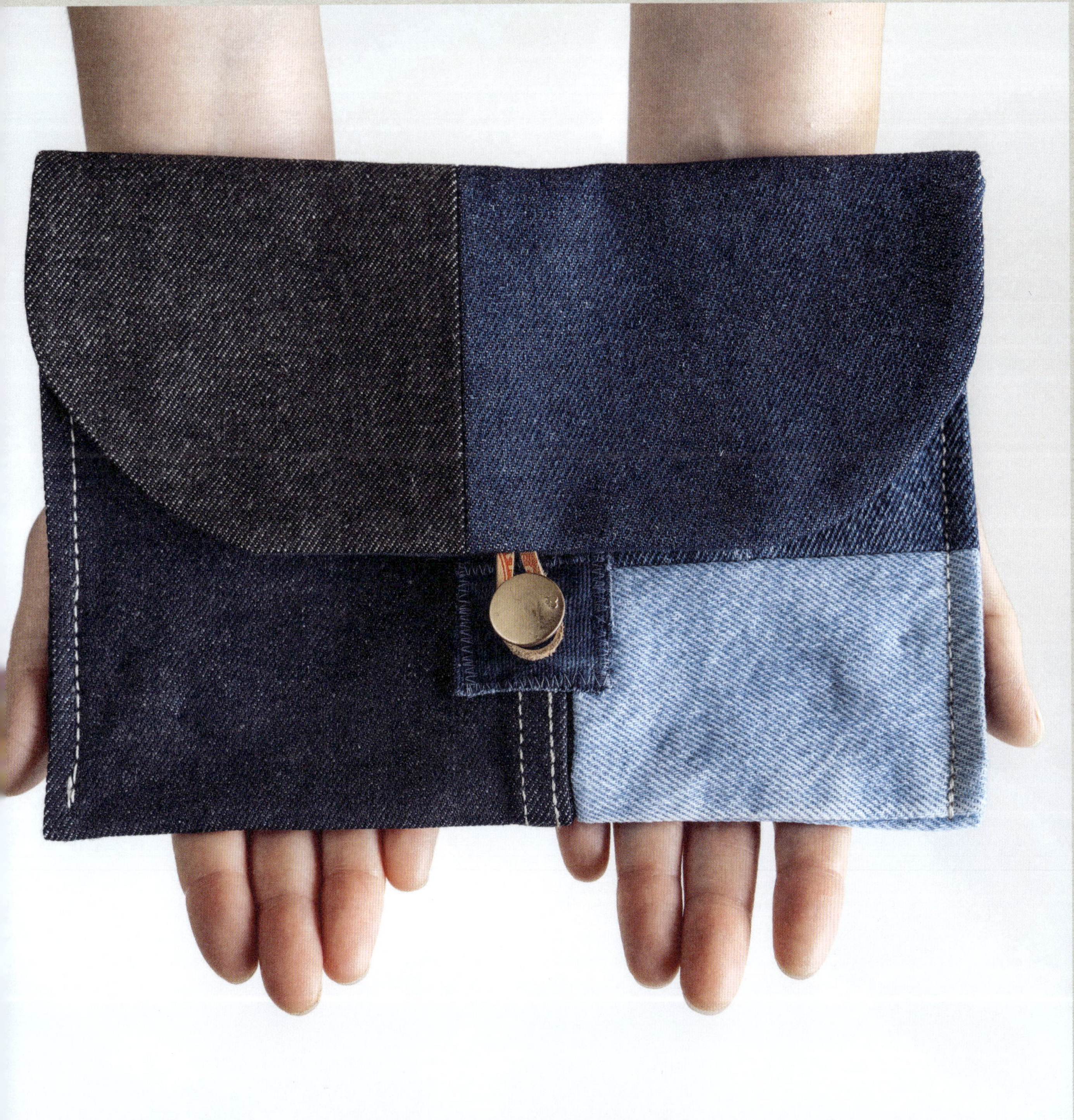

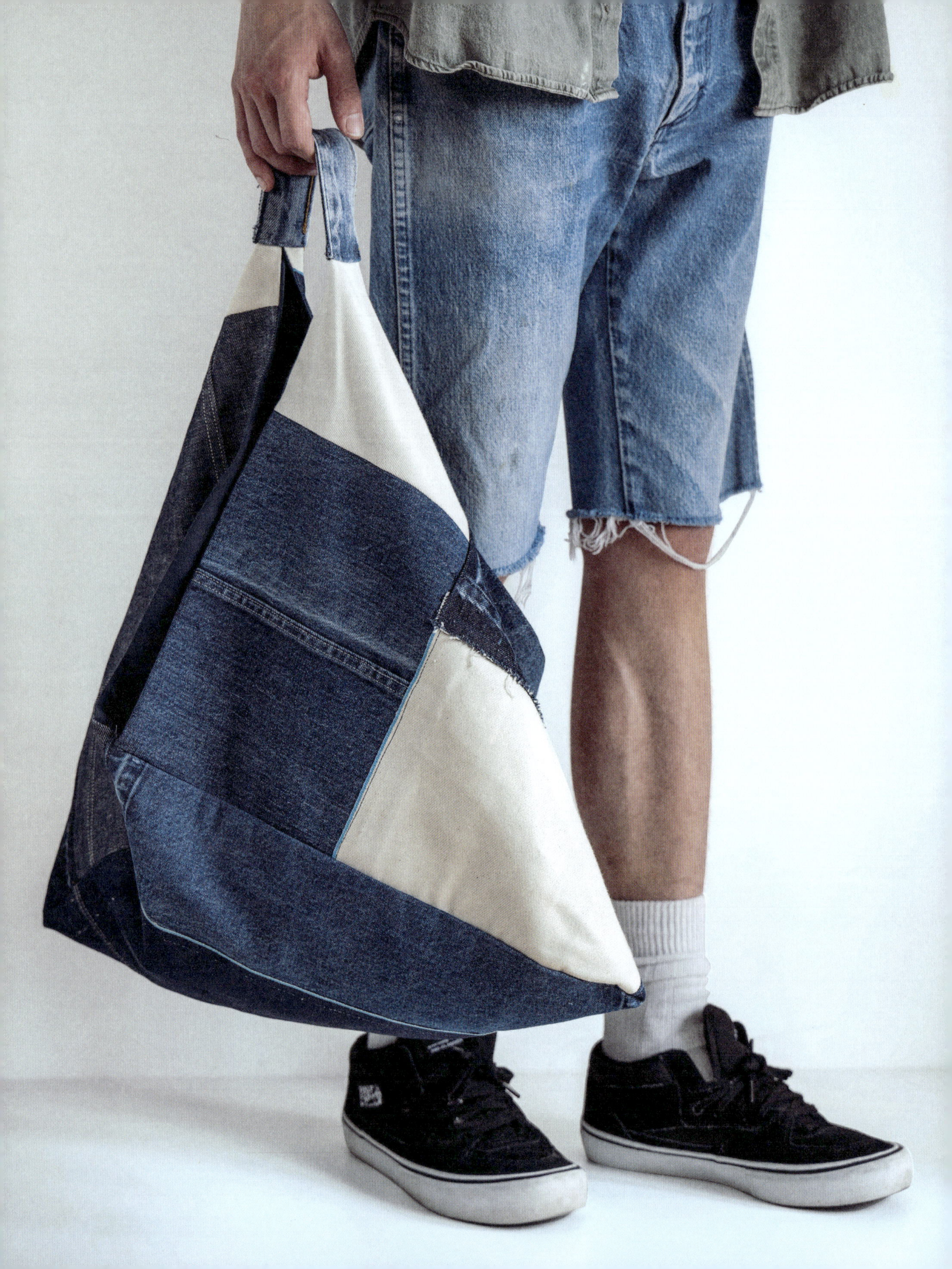

SKILL LEVEL	Basic
MAKE TIME	3 Hours
FINISHED SIZE	Approx. 60 × 50cm (23⅝ × 19⅝in)

PATCHWORK MARKET BAG

YOU WILL NEED

- Denim scraps or larger pieces equivalent to 150 × 50cm (59 × 19¾in) when joined together
- Section of waistband from an old pair of jeans for the handle, at least 12cm (4¾in) long
- 150 × 50cm (59 × 19¾in) lining fabric (a great way to use up an old sheet or pillowcase)
- Tape measure
- Fabric shears
- Sewing machine
- All-purpose threads
- Pins or sewing clips
- Tailor's chalk or fabric marker
- Steam iron
- Thread snips
- Seam ripper
- Scalpel

This striking triangular bag design comes from Japan, where it's been used for centuries and is known as the *Azuma* bag. The project uses the origami method to turn an upcycled patchwork panel into a stylish market bag. A waistband from an old pair of jeans makes the perfect handle.

Develop your bag design by adding jeans pockets in useful places or creating a closure using the button and buttonhole from the waistband.

1 Using your preferred patchwork style (see pages 149–153), create a panel measuring 150 x 50cm (59 x 20in). Cut a piece the same size from the lining fabric.

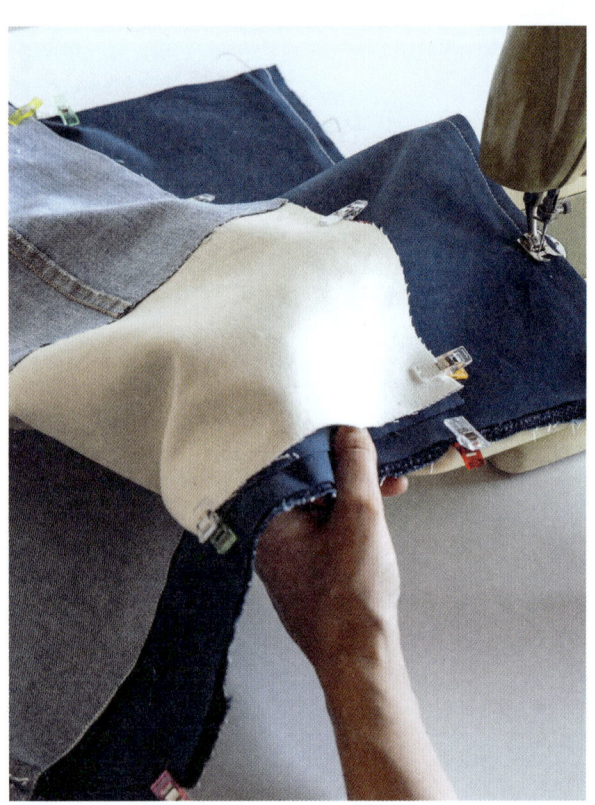

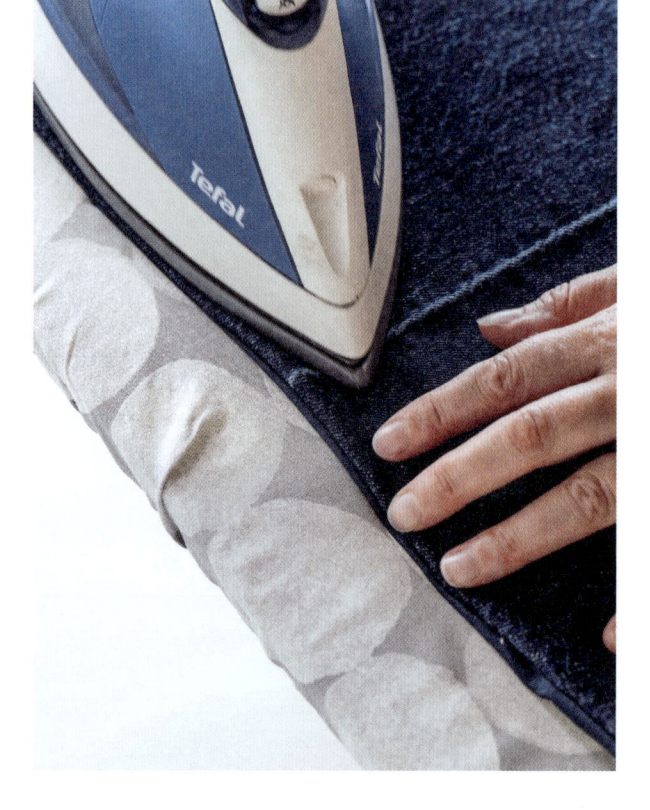

2 Clip or pin the patchwork panel and lining together with right sides facing and stitch around the perimeter, leaving a gap of around 10cm (4in) to turn it through.

3 Snip the corners, turn the pieces right side out and firmly press all the seams. Press the gap and close it with a topstitch.

4 With the right side facing up, lay the piece out horizontally on the table. Divide it into thirds and mark each third with chalk or a pin. Fold the right-hand section over the central section and run a line of stitching across the top.

5 Fold the bottom-left corner of the stitched section upwards towards the top-right corner to form a triangle.

6 Fold the left-hand half of the piece over the right, enclosing the turned up corner in the middle, then run a line of stitching across the bottom edge, parallel to the first stitch line.

7 Turn the bag inside-out and the shape will be revealed. Give it a firm press on the seams.

8 To finish the bag, add a handle salvaged from the waistband of some old jeans. Cut a section of waistband 19cm (7½in) long, removing the belt loops. Fold the ends of the waistband under 1cm (⅜in), press, then stitch along the long side, creating a tube.

9 Fold the points of the bag into an arrow shape and press.

10 Place the points as far inside the handle as possible (at least 4cm/1½in) and secure with a double row of topstitching. Repeat for the other side of the handle.

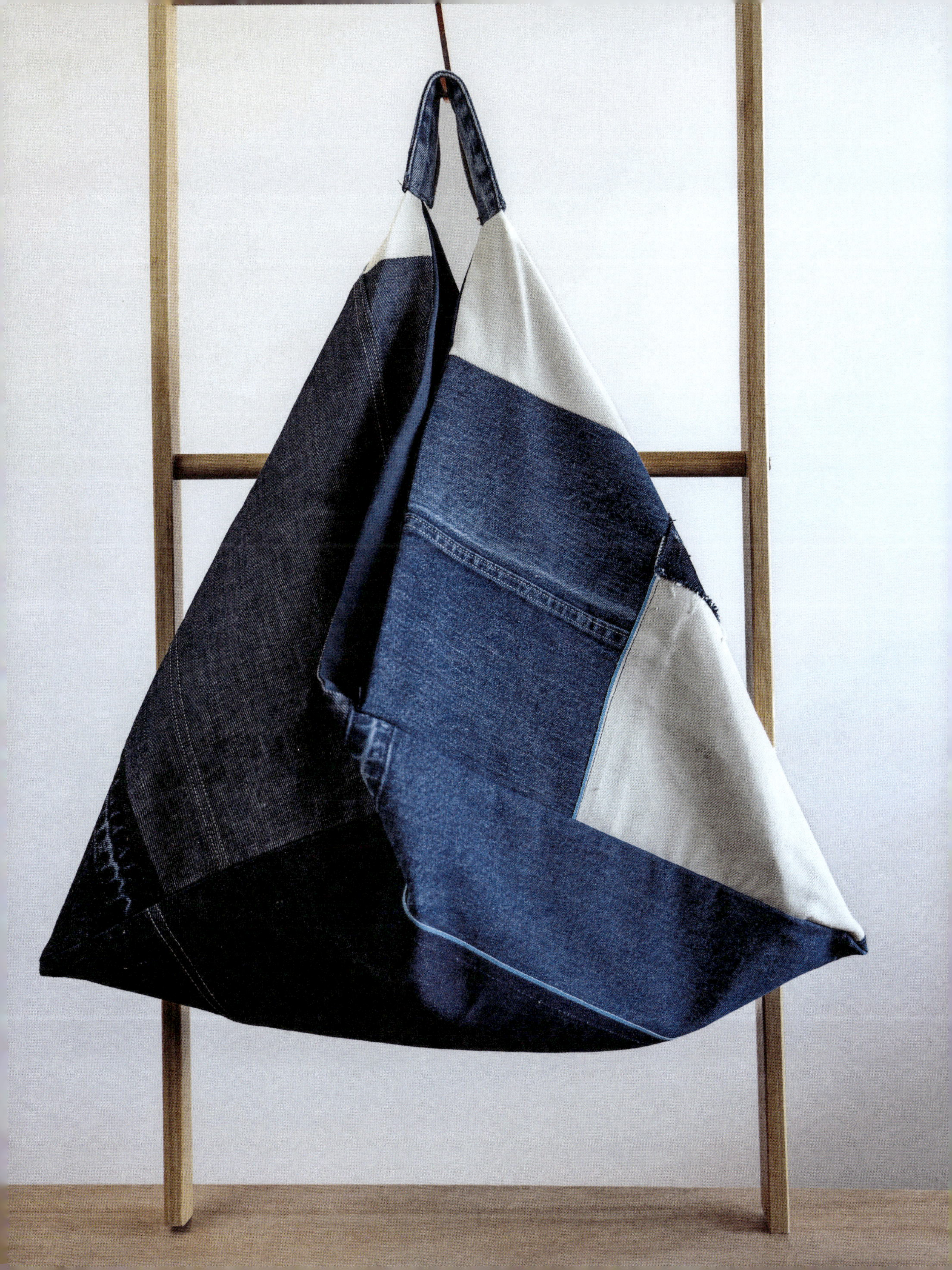

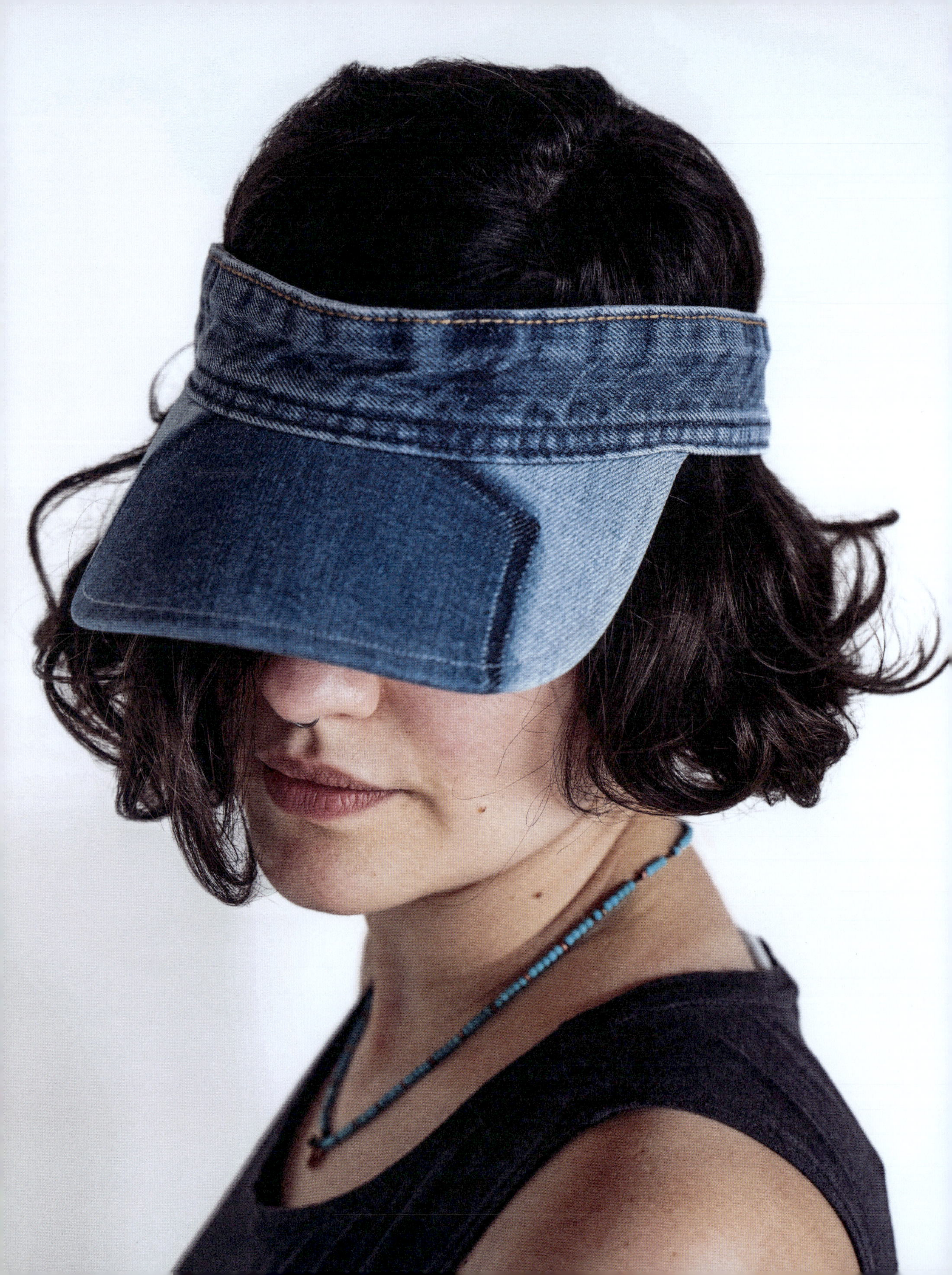

SKILL LEVEL	Medium
MAKE TIME	2 Hours
FINISHED SIZE	Made to fit your head

VISOR

YOU WILL NEED

- 1 jeans leg from knee down or equivalent scraps
- 49cm (19¼in) section of jeans waistband
- Unwanted or worn-out baseball cap
- 10cm (4in) length of 20mm (¾in) elastic
- Seam ripper
- 2 sheets of A4 paper, pencil and paper scissors
- Tailor's chalk or fabric marker
- Fabric shears
- Pins or sewing clips
- All-purpose threads
- Sewing machine
- Zipper foot
- Chopstick or point pusher
- Thread snips
- Steam iron

Fashion accessories are unlikely to be recycled due to the mixed materials used to make them. This innovative project uses waste that would otherwise end up in a landfill or incinerator, transforming a scruffy old baseball cap into a cool holiday essential with denim scraps and a piece of elastic.

1 Using the seam ripper remove the bill from the baseball cap.

2 Press the bill flat onto a piece of paper and draw around the edge, marking the shape. Don't include the seam allowance where the bill was joined to the cap.

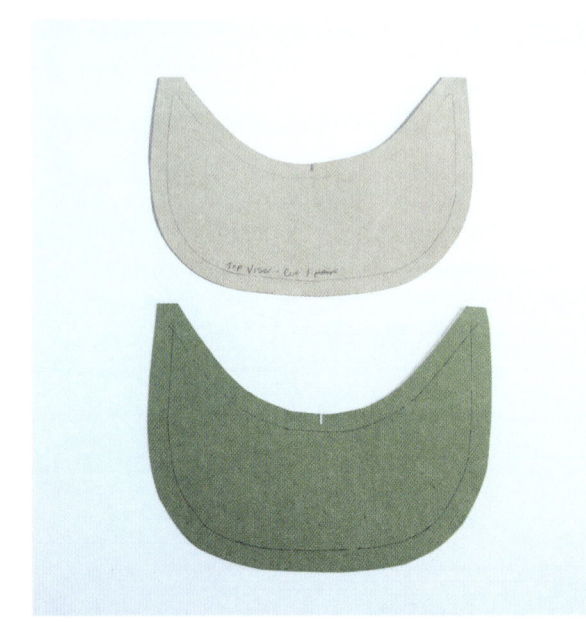

3 Use the bill outline as the bottom piece template. With pencil and paper, trace off another one for the top piece, 3mm (⅛in) longer on the outside edge than the original. Add 1cm (⅜in) seam allowance to all sides of both top and bottom and cut out both. Mark notches at the centre on the top edges of both.

If you don't have a tired old baseball cap to upcycle, reach out to your local charity shop and ask them to hold any unsellable baseball caps for you.

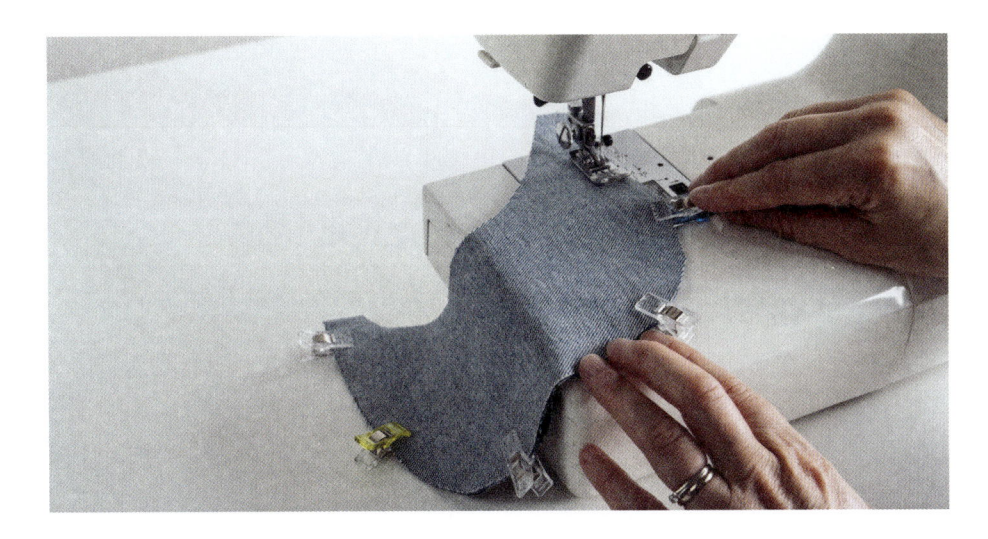

4 Cut out the upper and lower bill panels in denim. Place the right sides together, clip or pin them and stitch around the sides, leaving the top part open.

5 Press the seams to the underside of the bill. I find the easiest way to do this is to place the panels inside out over the bill and press the seams on the outside before turning it back in. Trim the seam allowance down to 5mm (3/16in) around the curve.

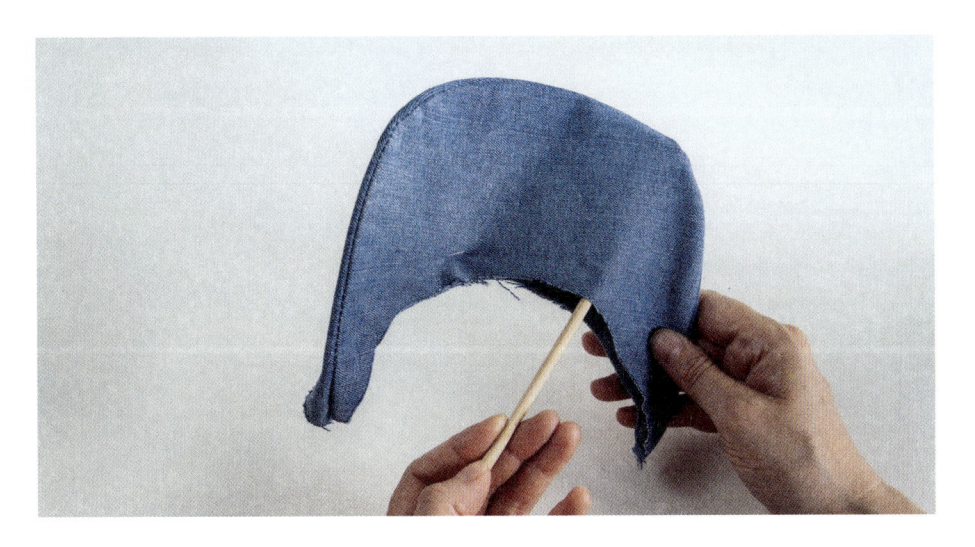

6 With the fabric the right way out, insert the bill into the denim casing, pushing the seam allowance to the underside of the bill with a chopstick or knitting needle. Use pins to hold the opening closed as you work. Patience is needed to get all the seam allowance positioned neatly on one side. Once in place, press firmly on both sides.

7 Pull the visor fabric taut and pin the top edge as close to the insert as possible. The amount of excess fabric may vary depending on how stretchy the denim is, but you should have at least 1cm (⅜in).

8 Using a zipper foot to get as close as possible to the bill, stitch along this edge to secure it. Trim the seam allowance back to 1cm (⅜in).

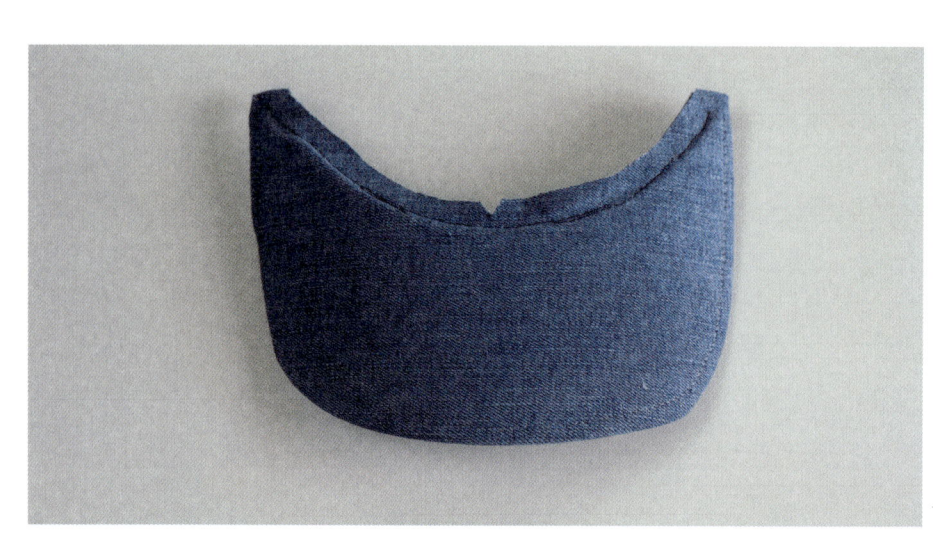

9 Finish with an edge stitch, a sewing-machine foot's width away from the outer edge, around the whole bill. If your machine struggles with several layers of fabric, try a sample first. If it doesn't work, skip this step. Cut a notch into the seam allowance at the centre of the bill.

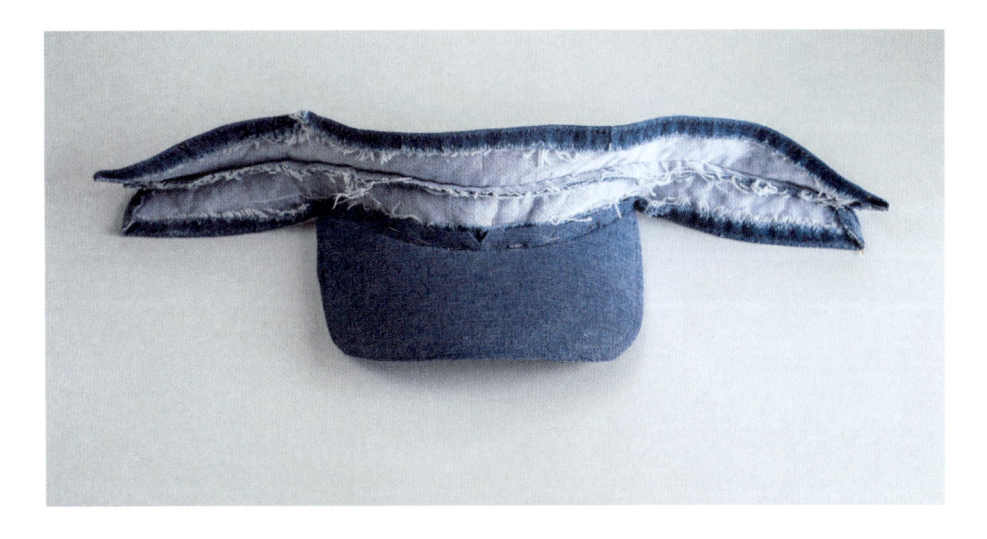

10 Prepare the jeans waistband by removing belt loops and turning the ends under by 1cm (⅜in). Leave the ends unstitched but press them firmly. Mark the centre with chalk. Line the centre up with the notch on the bill and secure with a pin before pinning the back side of the waistband to the underside of the visor, with right sides facing.

11 Using the zipper foot, stitch where you've pinned, trying to maintain the 1cm (⅜in) seam allowance and getting as close as possible to the insert.

12 Flip the topside of the waistband over and pin it in place at the front. Topstitch 2mm (¹⁄₁₆in) from edge, all around, to close the band, leaving the ends open to create a tube.

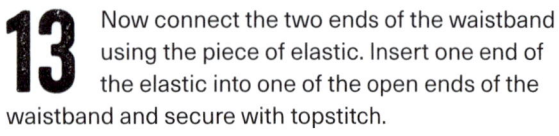

13 Now connect the two ends of the waistband using the piece of elastic. Insert one end of the elastic into one of the open ends of the waistband and secure with topstitch.

14 Take the other end of the elastic and insert at least 1cm (⅜in) into the other side of the waistband. Pin it in to begin with and test the visor for size, shortening the length of the elastic to fit if needed. When you are happy with the fit, close up the end of the waistband with topstitch, securing the elastic.

Old elastic from worn-out pyjamas or boxer shorts can be reused for this project. If yours doesn't look good enough to have on show, you can encase it in a denim tube as an alternative fixing at the back of the visor.

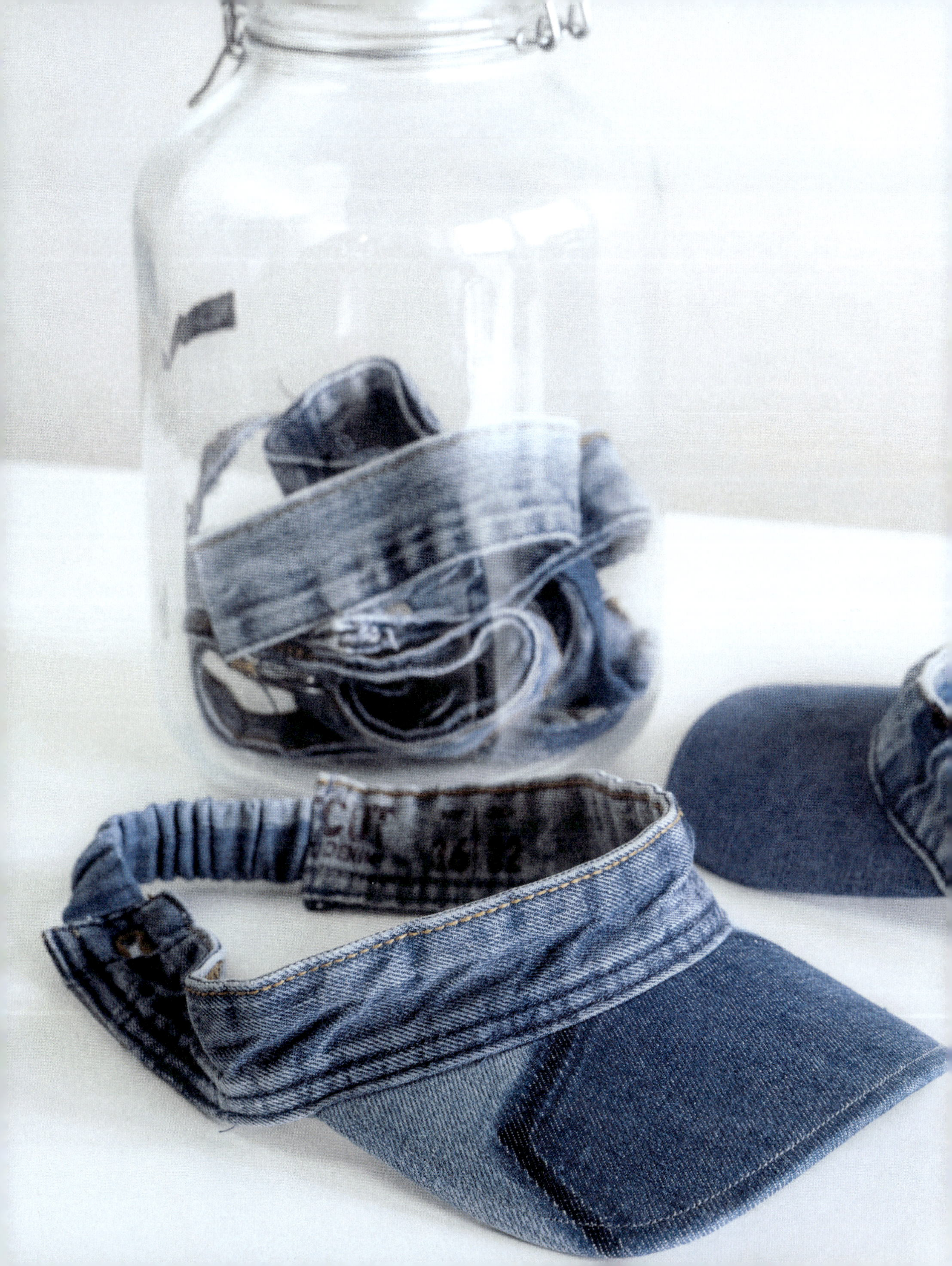

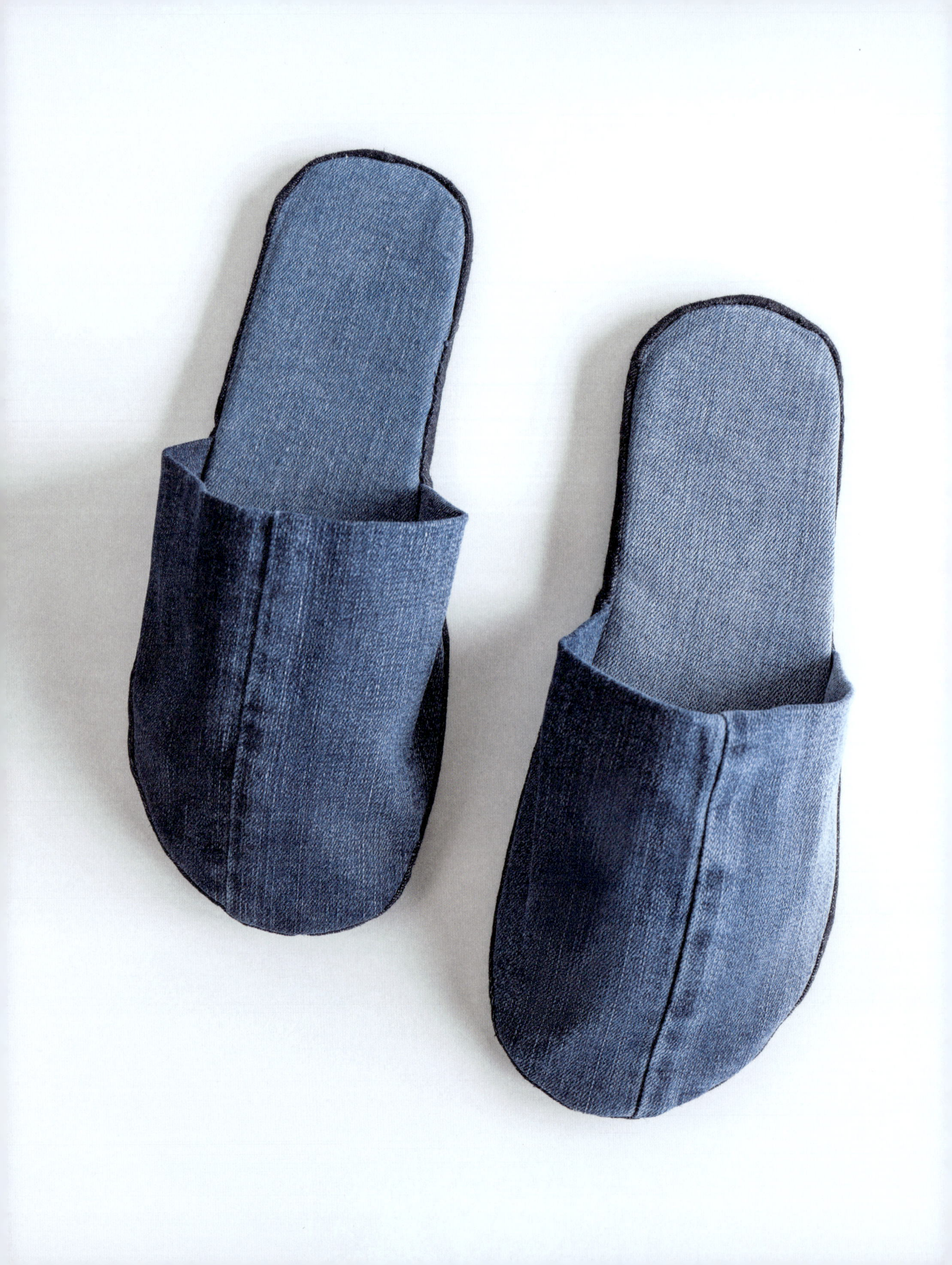

SKILL LEVEL	Medium
MAKE TIME	3 Hours
FINISHED SIZE	Made to fit your exact foot size

SLIPPERS

YOU WILL NEED

- 1 pair of stretchy jeans (or equivalent denim scraps)
- Towelling fabric – enough to layer double and cut two insoles from
- Pair of flip flops in the size you are making, or one size bigger
- Paper (or an old cereal box), pencil, ruler and scissors for making the pattern
- Pattern master or ruler with seam allowance
- Tailor's chalk or fabric marker
- Fabric shears
- Pins or sewing clips
- Sewing machine
- All-purpose threads
- Thread snips
- Chopstick or point pusher
- Steam iron

This attractive pair of slippers work best made with high-stretch denim. They are made up with an upper, a padding sandwiched between two layers of denim sole and a lining sole, which is bagged out and acts as a self-binding. Why not make a few pairs to keep by the front door to use as guest slippers?

DRAFTING THE PATTERN

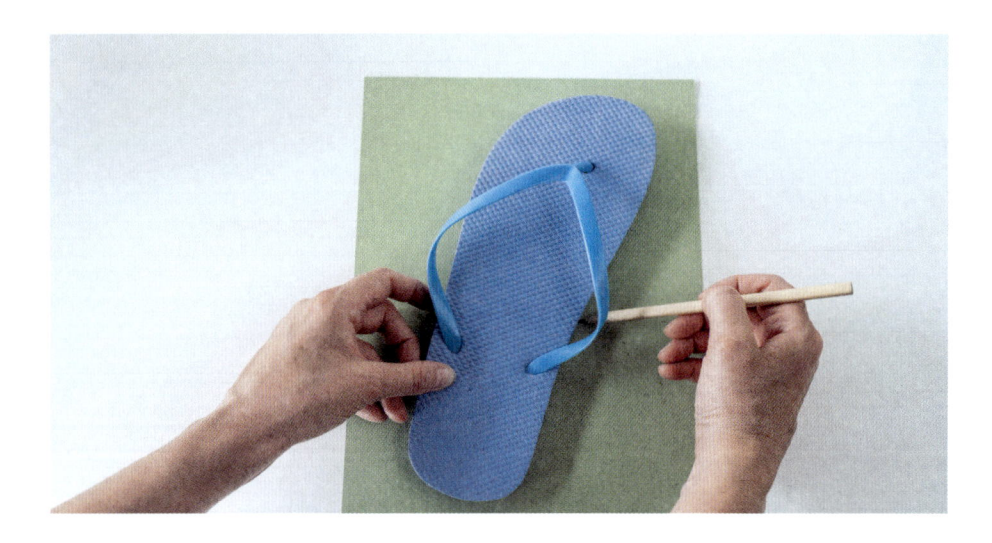

1 Draw around the left flip flop onto the piece of paper or card. Add a 1cm (⅜in) seam allowance all around the outer edge.

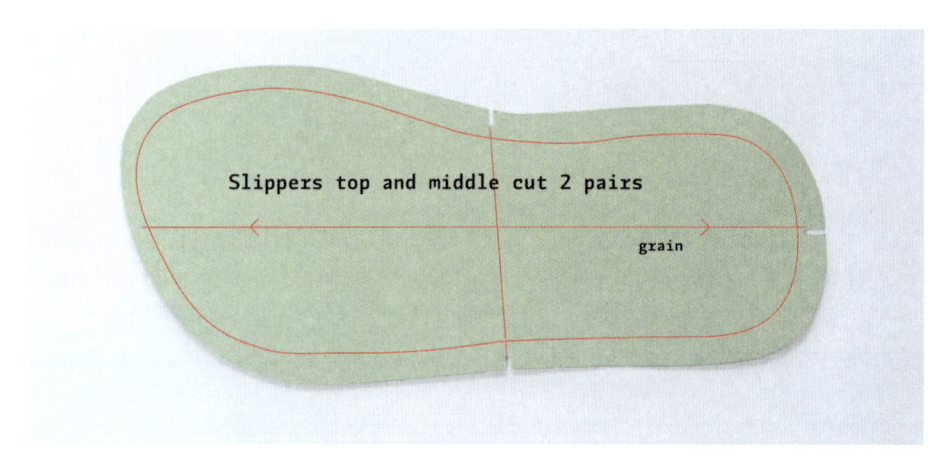

2 To create the pattern piece used for the top and middle parts of the sole, mark the point halfway vertically between the toe and heel. Draw a horizontal line 2cm (¾in) closer to the heel than the halfway point. Add notches at either side of this line. Add notches at the halfway points of the toe end and the heel end. Cut it out.

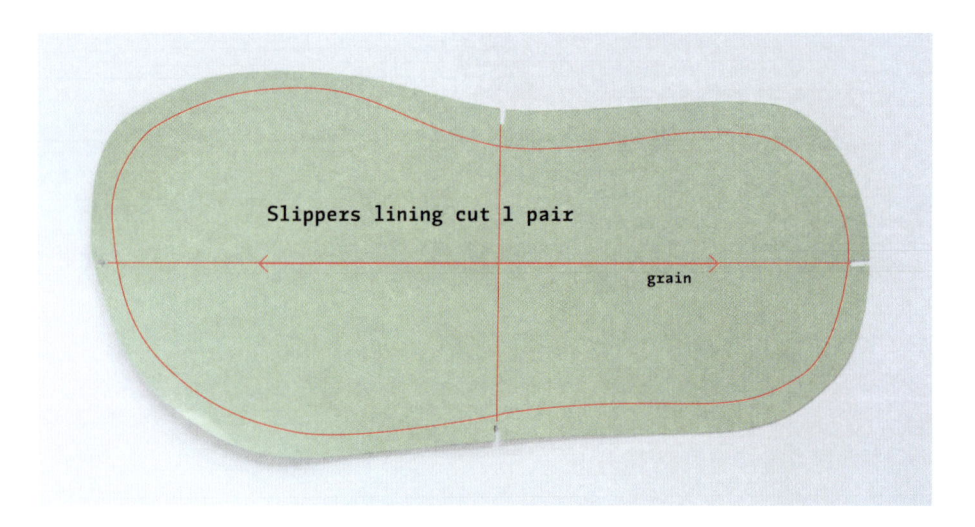

3 Draw around the pattern piece you have just made onto a new piece of card to create the pattern for the bottom part of the sole. Transfer the notches in the same position and then add an extra 5mm (³⁄₁₆in) seam allowance all around the whole piece. Cut the piece out. For both of the sole pattern pieces, the back side will be for the left foot and the front is for the right foot.

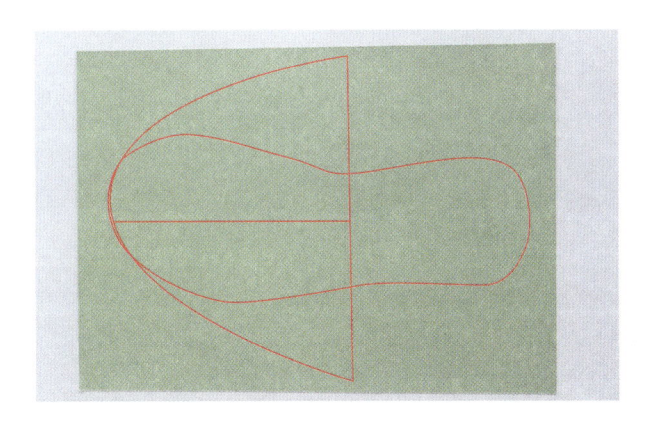

4 To create the upper pattern piece, measure the distance from the toe to the horizontal line. This will be the depth of the upper piece. To calculate the width, take the width of the sole at the widest point and multiply it by two. Draw the depth and the width onto paper or card, creating an upside-down 'T' shape. Place the left flip flop back on top of the paper and trace the shape of the toe (roughly from big toe position to little toe position). Draw a line to connect this curve to the side.

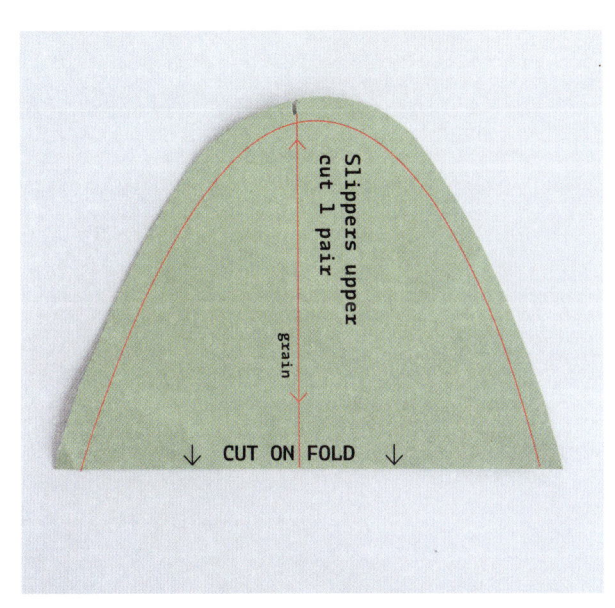

5 Check the distance from the centre notch to the end of the sides. The upper may be up to 1cm (⅜in) longer on each side of the foot than the sole, but if it is more, shave a little off your curve until the measurements are close enough. Add a 1cm (⅜in) seam allowance on the sides and write 'cut on fold' along the straight edge. Cut out the pattern piece for the upper.

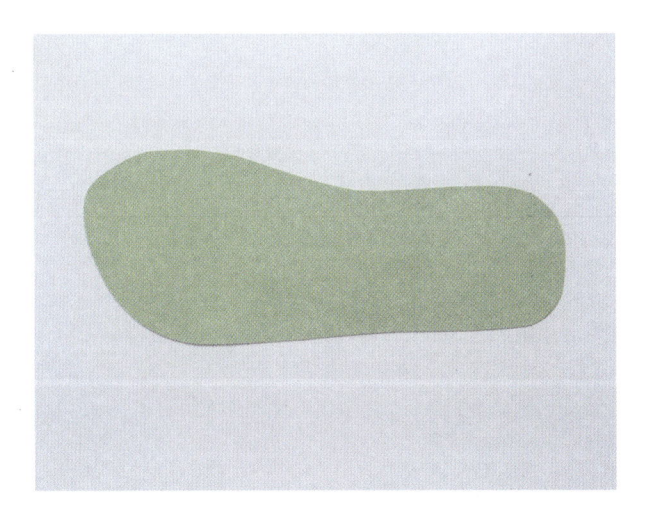

6 You will also need a pattern piece for the padded insole. To do this, draw around the left flip flop and, this time, do not add a seam allowance. Trim off 2mm (1/16in) all the way around when you cut it out.

> Mark all the paper pattern pieces with a grain line as the direction of stretch is important in this project.

7 Cut the pattern pieces from the fabric as follows:
Upper: Cut 2 in denim on the fold where shown. Avoid thick seams in the jeans you are cutting. Seams that are pressed open (often on the side seam) should be OK.
Sole (top and middle layers): Cut 2 pairs* in denim, avoiding all seams.
Sole (bottom layer): Cut 1 pair* in high-stretch denim.

Padded insole: Cut 1 pair* from double-layered towelling, roughly sewn together with a large zigzag stitch.
(*A pair = one front side and one back side of the pattern piece)

Transfer all the notches onto the cut-out pieces with chalk.

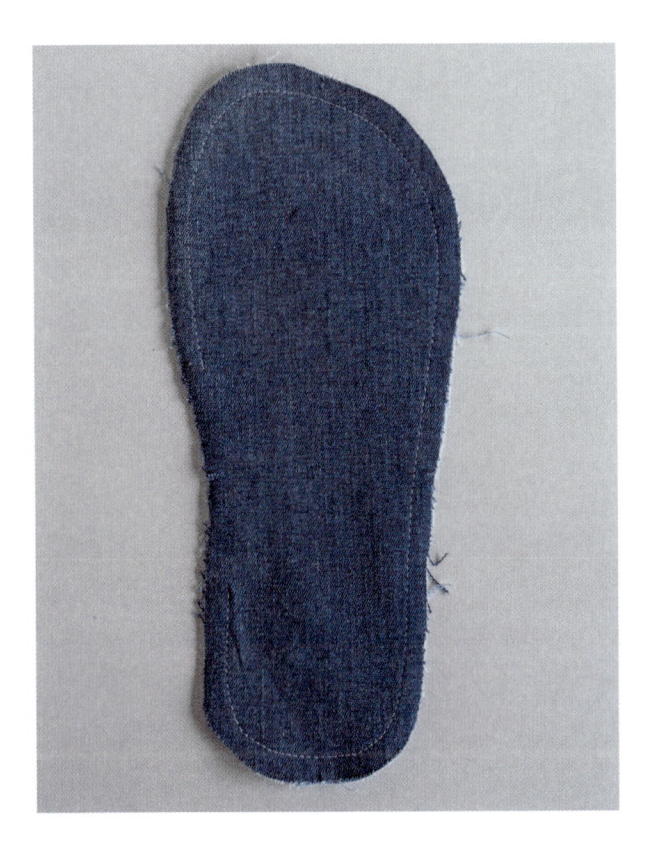

8 Pin the top and middle sole pieces together with wrong sides facing. Sew them together with a 1cm (⅜in) seam allowance. Leave an opening around 8–10cm (3–4in) long on the side.

9 Place the towelling insole inside the sole through the gap you left and then stitch it closed.

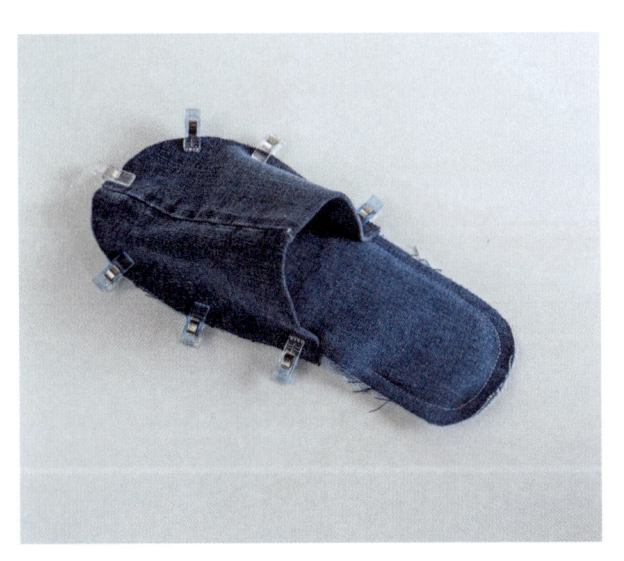

10 Pin or clip the upper to the sole, keeping the fabric folded. Match the notches, taking care to place the uppers on the correct foot.

11 Stitch around the edge using a 1cm (⅜in) seam allowance.

145

12 Now place the bottom sole piece with wrong side up on top of the upper. Pin or clip the pieces together matching the notches. The bottom piece is bigger than the rest of the sole, so you will need to stretch the slipper to fit the base.

13 Stitch the bottom onto the slipper with a 1cm (3/8in) seam allowance, leaving a gap 8–10cm (3–4in) on the side. I find it helpful to turn the slipper upside down and stitch over the top of the previous stitch line. As you are now sewing through four layers, stitch slowly and carefully.

14 Trim all the layers down to 5mm (3/16in) apart from the top one. Snip notches into the curve on the top layer.

15 Turn the slipper out through the gap, using a chopstick to push out the curve. Press the base firmly, turning the open edge under when you get to the gap. Finish by stitching the gap closed.

If you are confident with bias binding, you could finish your slippers by adding binding after step 11 and skipping steps 12–15.

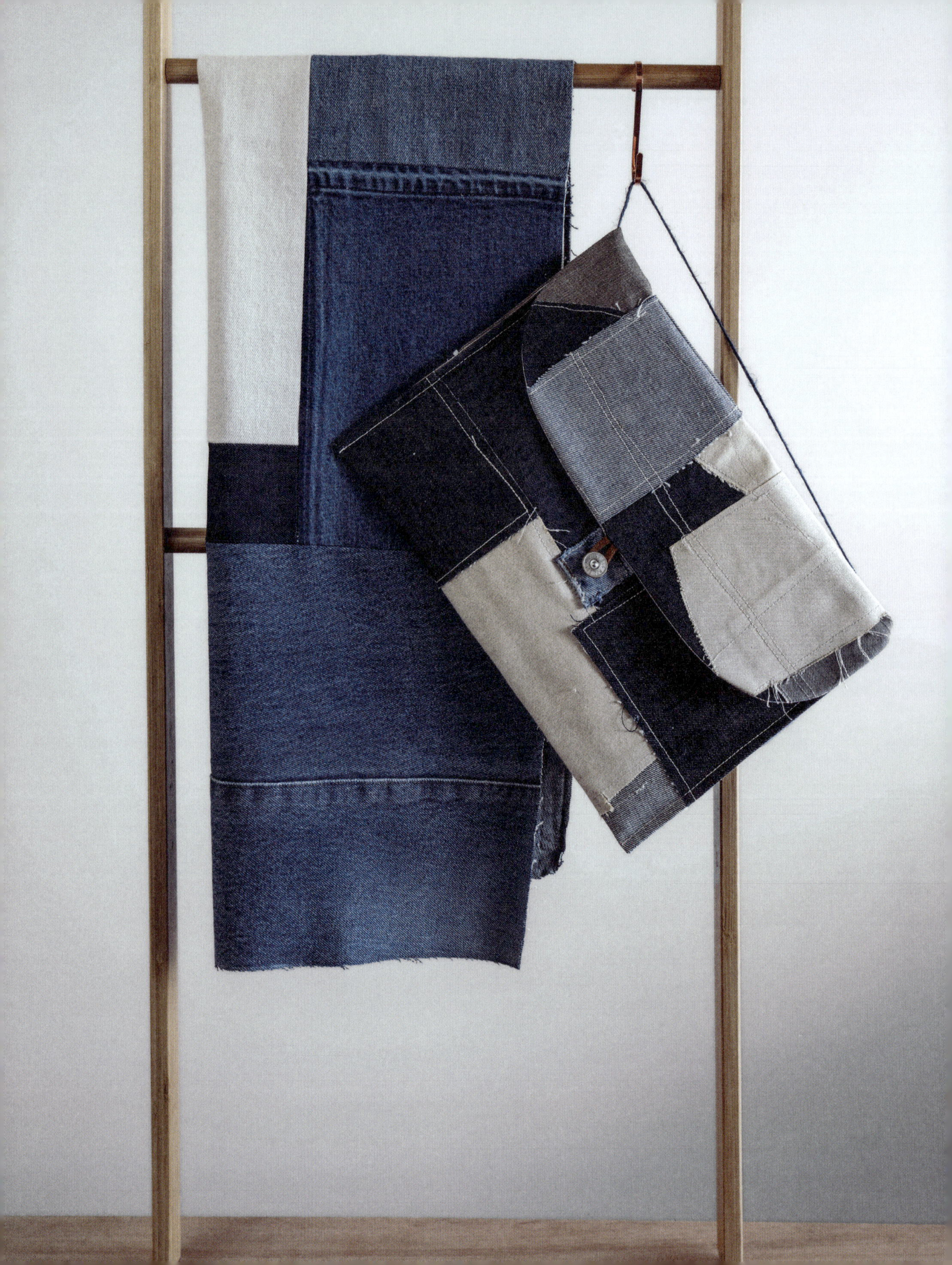

SKILL LEVEL	Easy
MAKE TIME	Depends on size of piece
FINISHED SIZE	Depends on size of piece

PATCHWORK

YOU WILL NEED

- Denim scraps
- Fabric shears
- Pins or sewing clips
- Tailor's chalk or fabric marker
- Ruler
- Sewing machine
- Heavy-duty topstitch threads

One of my favourite aspects of upcycling denim is creating patchworks. Small, forlorn pieces can become precious details when carefully reassembled, revealing a rich patina of textures and shades. Indigo patchwork has a global heritage spanning centuries – from the meticulously layered stitching of Japanese *boro*, to the graphic creativity of the quilters of Gee's Bend. These textiles are more than practical pieces of craftsmanship; they are woven with stories, history and experience.

In this section, you'll learn two easy methods to create your own indigo patchworks. The technique is just the starting point; the real artistry lies in the combination of colours and details. Save every scrap, experiment with tones and contrast, and try unpicking seams and pockets to reveal those bright indigo shadows.

PANELLED PATCHWORK

This method gives a clean finish. It can be as organised or as random as you prefer. Create the patchwork in strips and stitch them together, avoiding the need to join any tricky corners.

1 Prepare your denim scraps by cutting them into squares or rectangles.

2 Join pieces of a similar width into vertical strips. Press the seams to one side on the reverse then press again on the front.

3 Trim the pieces so that they have straight edges.

4 Pin or clip the strips together with right sides facing and then stitch on the sewing machine. Press the new seams firmly.

5 Repeat with more strips until you have a patchwork big enough for your project.

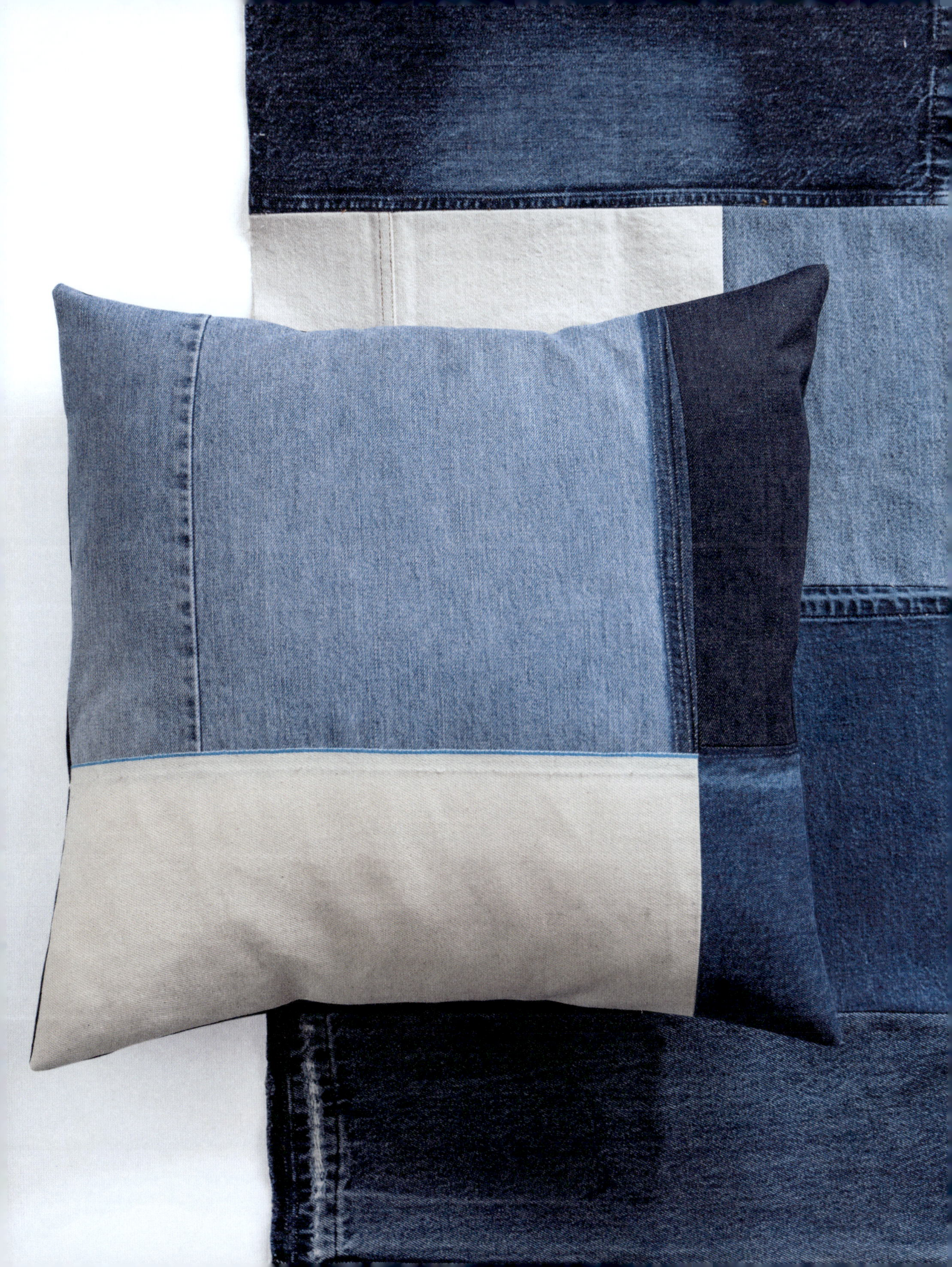

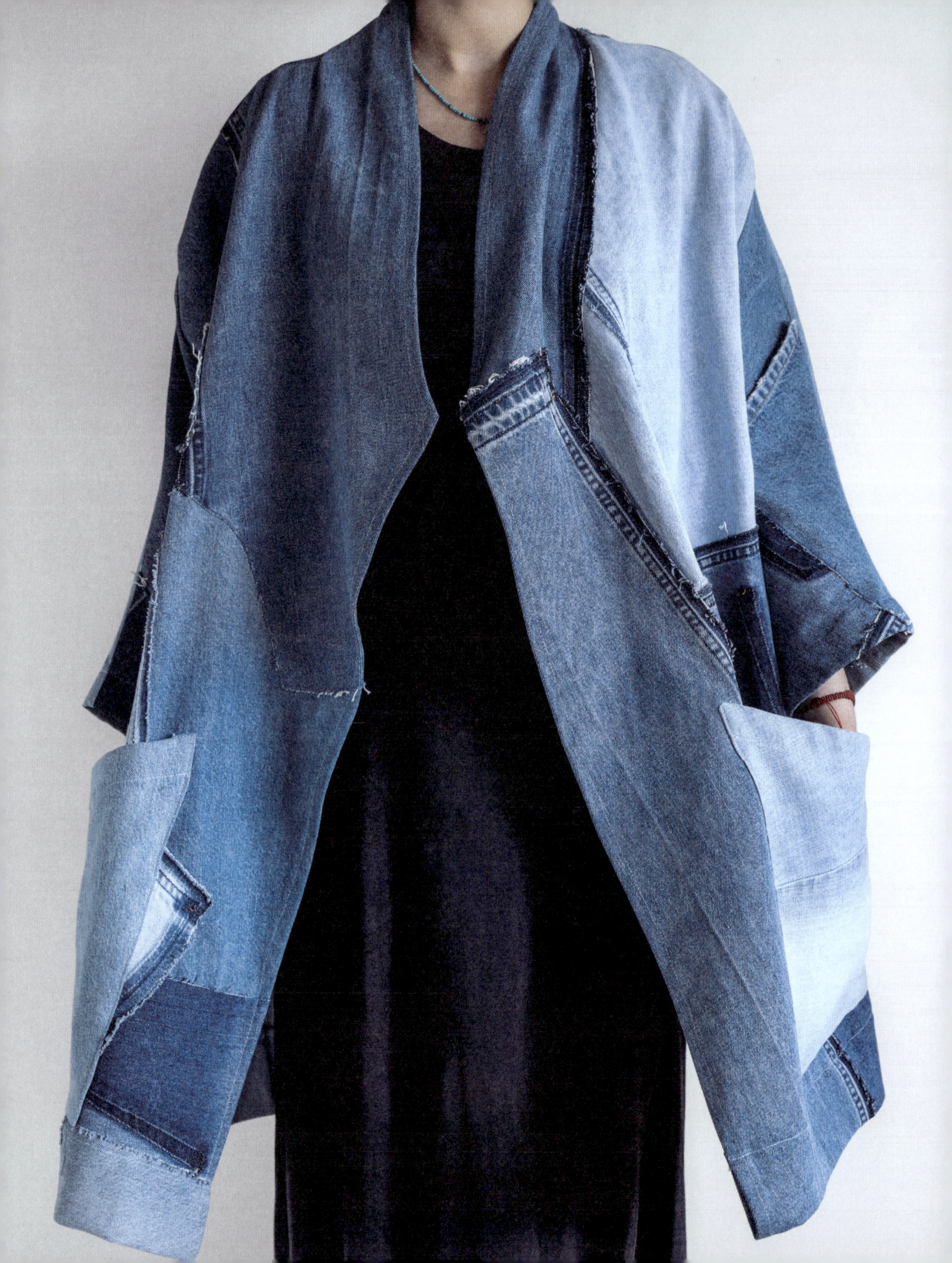

SCRAP COLLAGE

This is a fast and intuitive technique, perfect if you like a rustic upcycled aesthetic. The same technique works for scraps of any size – you can join whole legs or tiny offcuts.

1 Take your scraps pretty much as they are and arrange them by overlapping the edges. You'll want overlaps of at least 2cm (¾in); more is fine. Secure them with pins (the more you overlap, the easier it will be to pin). If you are making a very large patchwork, do this in sections.

2 Sew your scraps together by stitching about 5mm (³⁄₁₆in) from the edge of the pieces, on the right side, using a straight stitch. Try to sew in a continuous motion, without taking the panel off the machine. You can be very free with your stitch lines and run across scraps or do loops to get to the next piece.

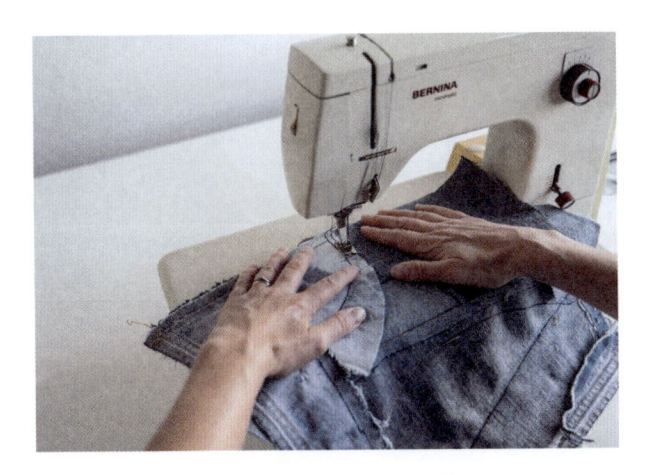

3 Next, turn your panel over and stitch down any loose edges. This will give you some interesting new lines on the front side. If you want to make a feature of it, you could use a different thread colour in the bobbin.

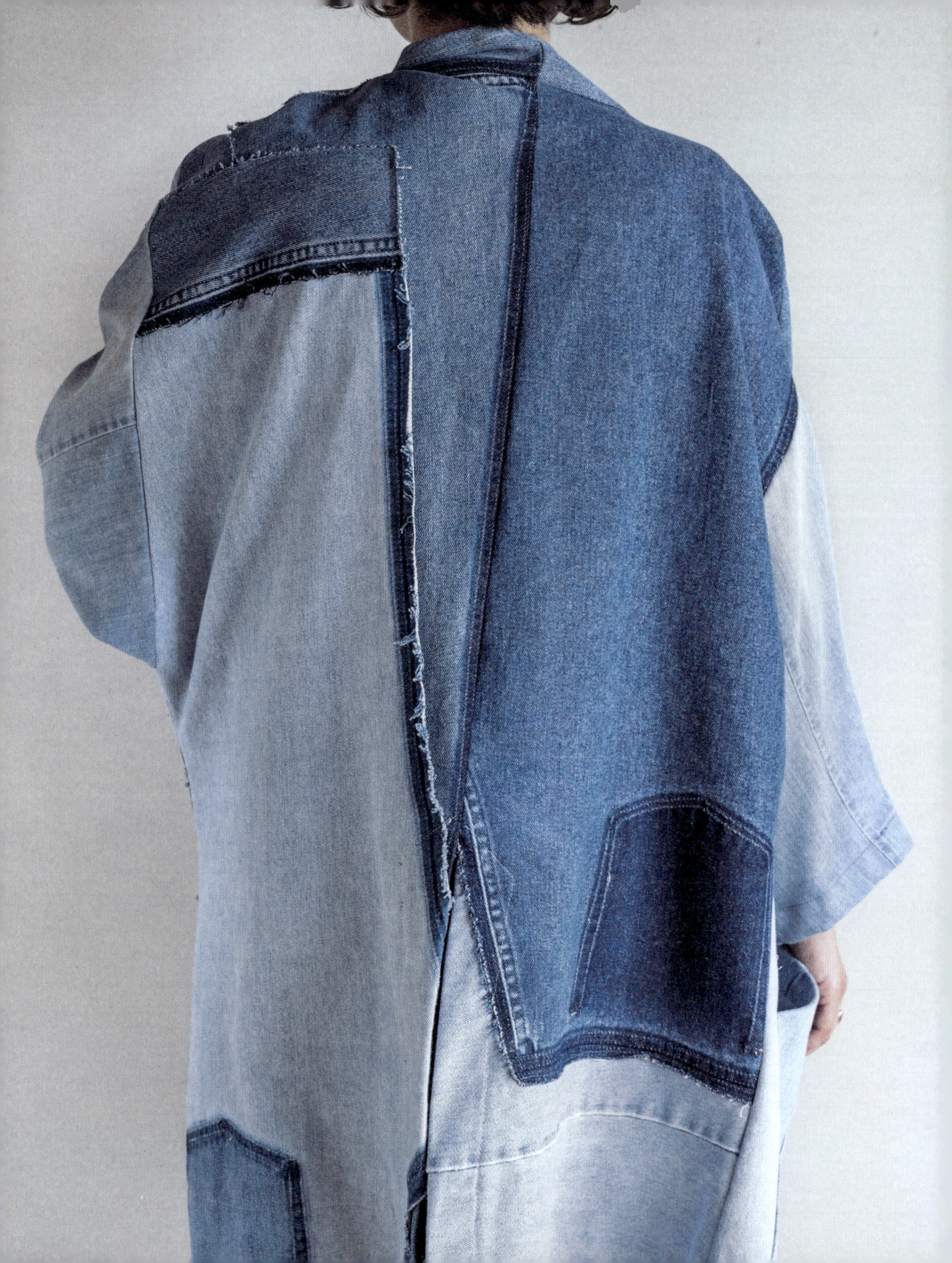

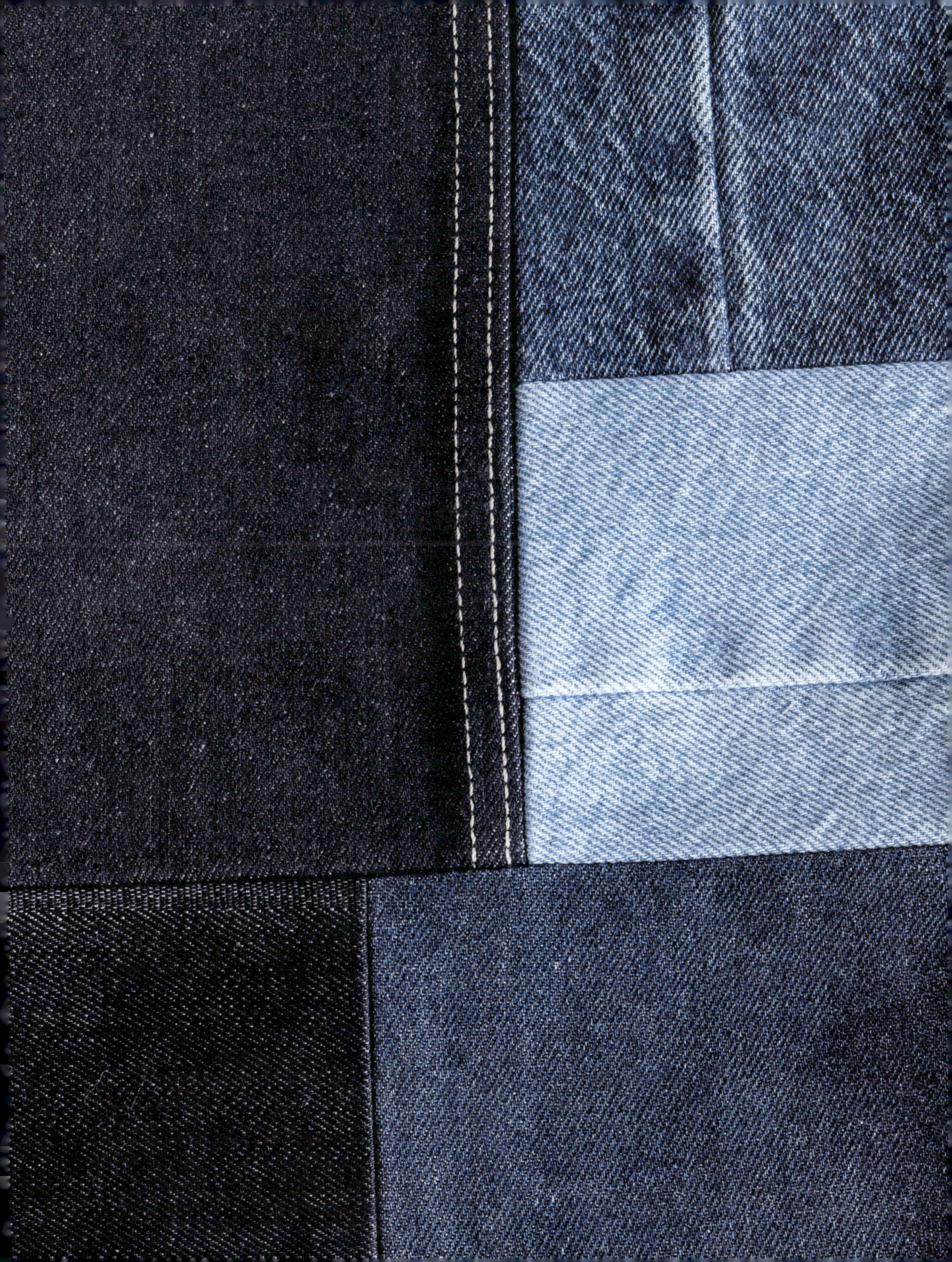

RESOURCES

BOOKS

DENIM KNOW-HOW
The Denim Manual: A Complete Visual Guide for the Denim Industry (Fashionary, 2022)

Indigo: The Colour that Changed the World, Catherine Le Grand (Thames and Hudson, 2013)

Indigo, Jenny Balfour Paul (British Museum Press, 2000)

HAND MENDING
50 Embroidery Stitches, Melanie Bowles (Stitch School, 2024)

Creative Mending, Hikaru Noguchi (Tuttle, 2022)

The Mending Directory, Erin Eggenburg (Search Press, 2021)

How to Train Your Sewing Machine, Rehana Begum (Skittledog, 2024)

UNPICKING FAST FASHION
Consumed, Aja Barber (Brazen, 2021)

The World is on Fire but We're Still Buying Shoes, Alec Leach (Future Dust, 2022)

Unraveled: The Life and Death of a Garment, Maxine Bédat (Portfolio, 2021)

Loved Clothes Last, Orsolo De Castro (Penguin, 2021)

WEBSITES

simplysuzette.com
Information about sustainable denim

Insidedenim.com
Denim industry innovation and news

denimhunters.com
Buying tips and knowledge for denimheads

WATCH & LISTEN

denimhuntermovie.com
An offbeat independent film about hunting for vintage denim

Inside the Factory – BBC One, Jeans: series 8, episode 3
A behind-the-scenes look at denim production

Wardrobe Crisis podcast
Discussing all aspects of sustainable fashion

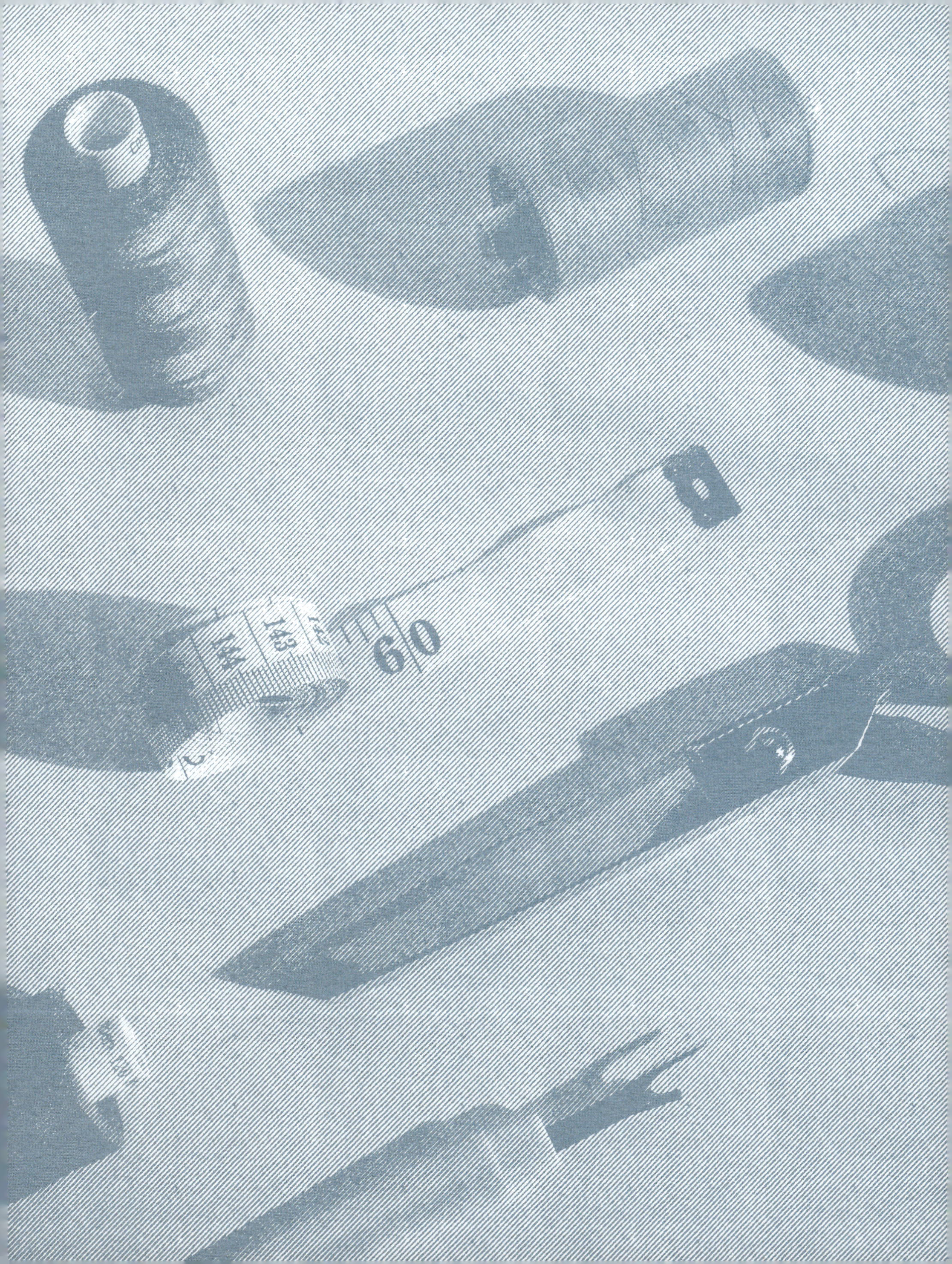
144
143
142
60

ABOUT THE AUTHOR

Janelle Hanna is a denim expert with a strong focus on eco-conscious design. With 15 years of experience designing for top brands like Wrangler, she has an in-depth understanding of denim production, which now informs her work in repair and upcycling.

In 2015, Janelle founded White Weft, a circular denim studio focused on reducing textile waste. White Weft creates stylish upcycled garments, innovative accessories, and precise repairs that redefine the value of pre-loved jeans. By challenging the fast-fashion mentality, Janelle's work encourages sustainable practices and shows that used denim can be just as desirable as brand new.

whiteweft.com
Follow on Instagram: @white_weft

ACKNOWLEDGEMENTS

A huge thank you to Madeleine Morgan, chief repairist and upcycler at White Weft, for patiently testing and sampling so many of the projects in this book. To our brilliant interns, Elodie Bennett and Shanice Animashaun – your hard work made all the difference.

Thanks to Fabric Floor for your generous support during the photoshoot and my deepest gratitude to Virginia Brehaut, Alison Guile, Zara Larcombe and the incredible team at Skittledog for your guidance and professionalism. Thanks also to our wonderful models Beril Nur Denli and Milo Larcombe, and to Charlie for the brilliant photography.

Finally, to Kyle, Rohan and Kit (our emotional support dog) – you're the best squad I could ask for – no more deadlines!

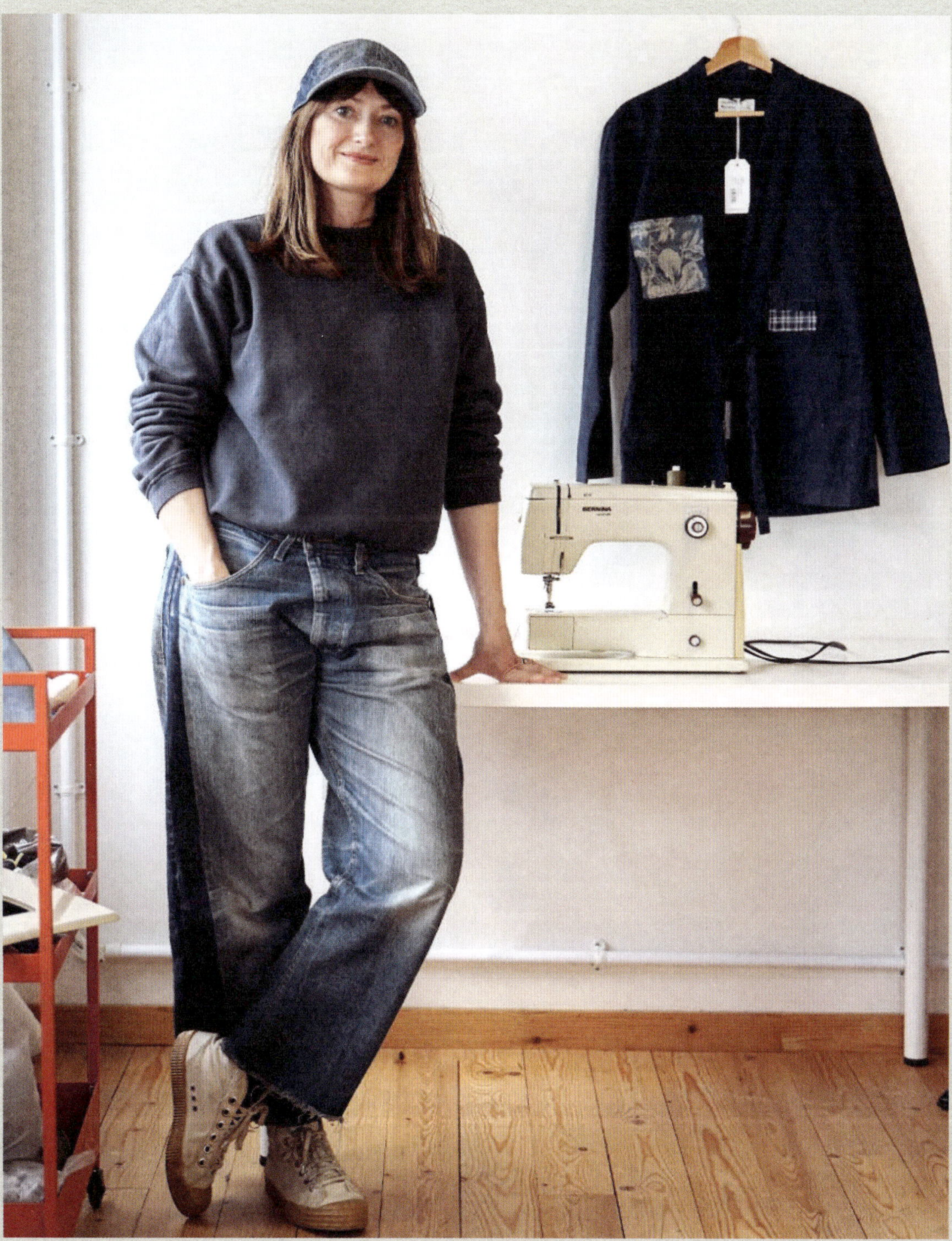

For Mum, to whom I credit my resourcefulness and Dad, fixer of many things.

Skittledog

First published in the United Kingdom in 2025
by Skittledog, an imprint of Thames & Hudson Ltd,
6–24 Britannia Street, London WC1X 9JD

Jean Genius © 2025 Thames & Hudson Ltd, London

Text © 2025 Janelle Hanna

Senior Editor: Virginia Brehaut
Designer: Alison Guile
Photographer: Charles Emerson
Production: Felicity Awdry

Additional photographs by: White Weft (pages 4, 67, 70–71 and 157); adobe stock.com, Ownza (page 10, top left), Danish Khan (page 13, both); Laurie Esdale (page 157); George Melton for Universal Works (page 159).

All icons from thenounproject.com, with thanks to1art, Alice Design, Amethyst Studio, Andrej Dvojkan, Azam Ishaq, Cahya Kurniawan, Candy Design, Dibichibi, Ex Liberus, Iconbunny, Icongeek26, Iconsparks, Indah Rusiati, Jang Jeong Eui, Kmg Design, Kokoto, Le Khac Bao Thoai, Marco Livolsi, Muhammad Atiq, Nattapol Seenge, Nawicon, ondon tv, ProSymbols, Sergey Demushkin, Smarty, Sugiman, Vectoricons, Vectors Point.

All Rights Reserved. No part of this publication may be reproduced or transmitted in any form or by any means, electronic or mechanical, including photocopy, recording or any other information storage and retrieval system, without prior permission in writing from the publisher.

EU Authorized Representative: Interart S.A.R.L.
19 rue Charles Auray, 93500 Pantin, Paris, France
productsafety@thameshudson.co.uk
www.interart.fr

A CIP catalogue record for this book is available from the British Library.

ISBN 978-1-837-76062-6
01

Printed and bound in China by C and C Offset Printing Co., Ltd

Be the first to know about our new releases, exclusive content and author events by visiting:
skittledog.com
thamesandhudson.com
thamesandhudsonusa.com
thamesandhudson.com.au